J. J. ENGLISH, S.J.: SPIRITUAL FREEDOM

English, J.J.   271.2051
                                 E 84 s
Spiritual Freedom

DATE	ISSUED TO
10/10/88	*[signature]*

Spiritual Freedom   271.2051
                        E 84 s
by J.J. English

Jesuit ~~High School~~ Library
1200 Jacob Lane
Carmichael, CA   95608

JOHN J. ENGLISH, S. J.

SPIRITUAL FREEDOM

FROM AN EXPERIENCE OF THE IGNATIAN EXERCISES TO THE ART OF SPIRITUAL DIRECTION

LOYOLA HOUSE
GUELPH, ONTARIO
1984

Dedicated to Paul Kennedy, S. J., St. Beunos College, North Wales. As Tertian Instructor Father Kennedy directed me through the Spiritual Exercises of St. Ignatius in October, 1962. His wisdom and inspiration then and in succeeding years are remembered with gratitude.

J. J. E.

Imprimi potest: Terence G. Walsh, S.J., Provincial of the province of Upper Canada, April 16, 1973. *Nihil obstat:* Michael G. Shields, S. J., Censor deputatus. *Imprimatur:* + Paul F. Reding, Vicar Capitular, Diocese of Hamilton, April 23, 1973.

Published by Loyola House, Box 245, Guelph, Ontario, Canada.
Printed by Good Books, Box 600, Cambridge, Ontario, Canada.

First edition 1973
Second edition 1974
Third printing 1974
Fourth printing 1975
Fifth printing 1977
Sixth printing 1979
Seventh printing 1982
Eighth printing 1983
Ninth printing 1984

PRINTED IN CANADA

CONTENTS

Preface   9

Introduction: Counseling and the Exercises   13

Chapter 1: Purpose of the Spiritual Exercises   29

Chapter 2: The Principle and Foundation   35

Chapter 3: Freedom and Commitment   45

Chapter 4: Directing Another's Prayer   56

Chapter 5: Sin and Salvation   69

Chapter 6: Personal Sin   87

Chapter 7: The Kingdom of Christ   106

Chapter 8: Discernment — First Week   124

Chapter 9: Contemplation — The Hidden Life   142

Chapter 10: The Two Standards   159

Chapter 11: Three Classes and Three Kinds   176

Chapter 12: Discernment — Second Week   190

Chapter 13: Choosing a State of Life   210

Chapter 14: Suffering with Jesus Christ   231

Chapter 15: Joy with Jesus Christ Risen   244

References   255

The reader may appreciate a brief explanation of how these pages came into being. Since their conversational style and somewhat circular form of presentation reflect their origin, a brief indication here of the needs I was initially seeking to satisfy and of the wider aims that later on led me to develop my ideas will perhaps help to give a clearer orientation to what follows. It is my impression that no other work on spirituality has attempted to achieve precisely these goals.

Each spring for four years (1969-1972) I conducted the Institute on Practical Asceticism at Loyola House, Guelph, Canada. This seven-week Institute began with the experience of the thirty-day Spiritual Exercises of St. Ignatius, personally directed on a daily one-to-one basis. The participants, some forty-eight in number, together with the team of seven priest-directors, then followed my lectures on spiritual counseling and entered into thorough discussion of the points raised. Since the 1971 lectures, questions and answers were taped, I have had the advantage of further in-put from later listeners, many of whom have urged me to make them available to a wider public. The tapes were transcribed, and some of the more important issues handled in discussion were then integrated with the talks themselves. The chapters that emerged were reworked and rewritten until they reached their present form.

The lectures were first intended to bring to the level of reflective awareness various spiritual movements which the participants had experienced in the thirty-day Exercises. I wished also to discuss the passages where these movements are indicated in the text itself of the *Spiritual Exercises of St. Ignatius Loyola.*[1] At the same time I was concerned to relate these personal developments to the basic ascetical principles of the spiritual life. The latter aim was in fact my primary concern because the participants were to be engaged in the spiritual direction of others both on retreat and outside the time of retreat.

In this way those who attended the Institute would gain a knowledge of these ascetical principles first through direct, personal experience and then through reflection upon that experience. I believe this experiential kind of knowledge to be most important for those giving spiritual counseling to others. Retreat directors not only need to know what they are talking about by having gone through it themselves but require as well a rather firm grasp of the fundamental principles. This is equally true for counselors who wish to prepare spiritually minded persons for an extended retreat or to direct them in their daily lives after they have undergone a prayer experience of some depth.

I am not alone in my conviction that the thirty-day Exercises of St. Ignatius incorporate a truly remarkable range of spiritual principles. Of course, some of the special points made by Ignatius are designed solely for prayer experiences in time of retreat and would not apply to spiritual counseling outside the thirty-day Exercises. Accordingly, I have attempted to distinguish these factors by indicating the significance of Ignatius's words for prayer and decision-making both within and outside a retreat situation.

This book is intended, therefore, for those who have had a personally directed experience of the Exercises and wish to deepen their understanding in order to give spiritual counseling to others. It will also be helpful to those who direct the Exercises, but it is not detailed enough to be a complete manual for this purpose. It may be useful to those who are familiar with the *Spiritual Exercises* and wish to understand its significance in our existentially and psychologically orientated world. Moreover, some persons who have made the Exercises may wish simply to deepen their spiritual life by reflecting upon the principles discussed here.

This book is not a technical treatise on the *Spiritual Exercises of St. Ignatius Loyola,* such as one might expect from an historian, an exegete, a theologian, a psychologist or a linguistic analyst. Nor is it a handbook for counseling. There is not enough detail about interviewing techniques and other counseling procedures for that. Nor is it a scholarly study of the different sections of the *Exercises* or of ascetical principles found in it. I have referred to many such studies and scholarly works and have relied a great deal on them, but my present aims are personal and practical and the language I use is rarely technical.

I might say that this treatment of the *Exercises* is more phenomenological than those just mentioned. It describes the experience of those participating in the personally directed *Spiritual Exercises* of Ignatius. In some instances it inquires into the exercitant's personal experience. But, for the most part, it considers the director's experience as he shares in the movements which his exercitants undergo and as he strives to help them follow the lead of the Holy Spirit. If it does not sketch these relationships with the Holy Spirit in fine detail but rather in larger strokes, there is an excellent reason: each person receives unique knowledge of the Spirit both when making and when directing the Exercises.

This study has emerged from three kinds of experiences: from my own repeated experience of the Exercises, from directing many exercitants through the thirty-days and hearing them

11

describe what happened to them, and from reflections on my experience as a director. It is also the result of prolonged discussion with many wise directors who have undergone the same three kinds of experience.

I would like to express my special gratitude to Father Tom Walsh, S.J., of the New York Jesuits, who spent many weeks in discussion with me in an effort to clarify the points I wished to make and to give them clearer expression in written form. Truly this book could not have been written but for his generous and insightful help.

Father John Wickham, S.J., has spent many hours reading and correcting the language of the text. He and the Guelph Community of Jesuits deserve special thanks for their constant dialogue with me on the *Exercises* and the encouragement they have given to the publishing of this book.

INTRODUCTION

COUNSELING AND THE EXERCISES

The word of God is something alive and active: it cuts like any double-edged sword but more finely: it can slip through the place where the soul is divided from the spirit, or joints from the marrow; it can judge the secret emotions and thoughts. (Heb 4:12)[2]

After undergoing thirty days of intense prayer in the Spiritual Exercises of St. Ignatius, especially when a personal director was available every day to hear what was happening to you in prayer, to ask you questions and to suggest new topics for reflection, you emerge from the whole experience with — at the very least! — a larger view of the spiritual life as a whole. The book of the *Exercises,* it may be said, deals with all the basic human responses to the triune God.

Of course, there is no substitute for the uniquely individual experience you have gained in confronting the merciful love of the Father, in receiving the powerful invitations of Jesus Christ, his Son, and in feeling the mysterious movements inspired in your inmost heart by the Holy Spirit. In fact, too many Christians speak of these matters out of purely conceptual knowledge and not from personal experience of sinful attachments, of struggle, of fear and withdrawal, of surrender and sorrow and renewed confidence, of self-deceptions and self-oblations and all the rich capacities of human love.

But when you have actually undergone this whole range of

responses, it is natural to feel that what you have received would be valuable for others too. God's gifts are truly meant for us, and yet, through us, they are meant for other members of his Body. Emerging from the experiential knowledge of many individuals are the mysterious ways of God with man. Embedded in the Exercises which St. Ignatius made so practical for modern persons, I am convinced, are many crucial principles of the spiritual life that could be clarified and deepened in us during the months and years that follow our great experience of the Lord.

These ascetical principles, if we can grasp them with fidelity, can also guide those who direct others through the Exercises, who wish to prepare some individuals to approach the Exercises, or who are asked to give spiritual counsel to people struggling with everyday problems of Christian life. But it is not a highly abstract, logically connected set of principles (expressed in a rigorously technical language) that will serve these purposes well. At every stage in this work, therefore, an effort will be made to adhere closely to the precise prayer-experiences, known individually to many, designed by St. Ignatius and set forth in his little book.

There is, of course, a considerable difference between the direction one receives when going through the thirty-day Exercises and direction one should give or receive outside that experience. This difference is kept in mind throughout the following pages, and it will be mentioned distinctly as occasions suggest. And yet, one who has experienced the personally directed Exercises can now reflect and relate his experience to the basic ascetical principles that are useful in all spiritual counseling. The following pages will try to highlight these ascetical principles as they were presented and experienced in the Exercises and indicate when they are most useful in counseling, whether within or outside a retreat situation.

What this book is about is the gaining of spiritual freedom.

This central theme will become more obvious as the book progresses (it receives special treatment in Chapter 3). But from the start it is essential to note that spiritual freedom involves the whole person: it penetrates the biological and the psychological spheres of existence as well as the spiritual.

Normally one does not speak of biological freedom but rather of a healthy or an unhealthy body. But even apart from medical factors a person can at times experience in himself or see in others a physical exhilaration or vitality (consider, for example, dancing or gymnastics) that amounts to an increasing freedom when it is present and slows one down all too noticeably when it is missing. It is much more common, of course, to speak of psychological and of spiritual freedom.

To the extent permitted by biological limitations, both psychological and spiritual counseling try to move the client towards the ideal of full interior freedom. The psychologist hopes to bring him to the deeper understanding of his whole self revealed in his historical background as it bears, both consciously and unconsciously, on his present existence. The spiritual counselor, while he may also be concerned with that kind of self knowledge, depends primarily on the loving and forgiving activity of divine grace (the operations of the triune God).

Perhaps the basic difference between the two kinds of counseling can be expressed as follows. Psychological counseling aims to bring a person to greater freedom through natural self-knowledge. Spiritual counseling aims to bring him to greater freedom through the experience of God's forgiveness.

Although it may be helpful for the director to distinguish between psychological and spiritual counseling, these realities are not distinct within the person being counseled. And our concern is always with the total person. We are not interested merely in some isolated dimension of an individual, such as his soul or emotions or intellect, but in the integrated person.

I think you can consider a human being as a union of three areas, the biological, the psychological, and the spiritual. As I understand it, the psychological includes the biological. The spiritual includes both the psychological and the biological. (There is, as you know, a new discipline emerging which is called «psychotheology.» It studies the relationships between the psychological and the spiritual.)

There are all kinds of neutral actions taking place in our being and in our interpersonal relationships with other human beings; for example, all our biological activities are beyond our control, and all our emotional reactions come upon us unexpectedly. These are neutral and in themselves neither good nor bad. They become good or bad insofar as the will and spirit use them for beneficial or for hateful reasons.

Of course, a spiritual counselor should be conscious of the biological influences on a person as well as of the psychological and spiritual ones. Perhaps the person's tension or lethargy is a result of bad diet or thyroid deficiency, or a need for new glasses or a hearing aid, or lack of exercise and sleep. As you cannot put a spiritual band-aid on a psychological disorder, neither can you put a psychological band-aid on a biological disorder. It is true, however, that the need for regular medical checkups is widely accepted today, and I will not emphasize the point any further in this book. But the biological and emotional reactions may be indicative of deeper disorders, first on the psychological level and then on the spiritual level.

Spiritual direction, it seems to me, can help the counselee discover whether or not this is so. For example, the counselee may be convinced at first that his troubled reaction to others is due to an ingrained sense of inadequacy resulting from events in his

16

family background (the psychological level). But with prayer and a more relaxed introspection he may discover that an egotistical motive is influencing his behavior (the spiritual level). For example, he may desire to dominate the situation and to manipulate other persons.

If that is the case, then he longs to be God and refuses to accept his creaturehood, or else he lacks gratitude for the gifts God has given him. Through spiritual direction the counselee can get to the deeper causes of his anxiety and thus be healed by the grace of God's love. All this can take place only in a prayer context, for only in the interpersonal exchange with the Trinity can man find his full integrity.

In as much as the distinction can properly be made, the God dimension enters more fully into spiritual than into psychological counseling. The awareness demanded is more than self-awareness; it is 'other-awareness' and awareness of «The Other.» In psychological counseling two persons are relating to each other. But in spiritual direction both the counselor and the counselee should be listening to the Trinity as the divine Persons enter into the life of the counselee.

In psychological counseling one is more directly involved in the intrahuman dimension; for example, in the events of one's early childhood and adolescence. In many instances the period of early childhood is extremely important in psychological counseling, especially that time before the child has heard of God. More generally, the complex of results on the intrahuman dynamics, if I may use this expression, is the main concern in psychological counseling. But in spiritual counseling the God-with-man area becomes dominant.

Now, obviously, one's relationship with God is going to determine, and be determined to a notable extent, by one's intrahuman relationships. One's image of God, say, as a Santa

Claus or as a policeman, colors all intrahuman relationships. And hatred for one's father can complicate one's approach to the fatherhood of God. Psychological counseling aims primarily at improving a person's relationships with other men; incidentally, this might enable him to reach a new conception of God. In contrary fashion, spiritual counseling should help a man to achieve a truer relationship with God, and this would likely affect the whole range of his human contacts.

Again, both psychological and spiritual counseling must deal with guilt. A psychologist would be concerned about a neurotic guilt complex and would try to remove the complex. But in spiritual counseling the counselor needs to discover whether or not the guilt experienced by the counselee is true guilt. When there is true guilt, the function of spiritual counseling is to make the person aware of the kindness of God and lead him to a true relationship with Him. If the guilt is neurotic, the spiritual counselor may refer the counselee to a psychiatrist or psychologist and, in the meantime, help him to live with this cross. If I am not mistaken the problem of human guilt is more complex than this for it involves one's solidarity with the guilt of the whole human race, but I shall return to the question in a later chapter.

Some of the techniques of psychological counseling are an aid in spiritual counseling, especially such non-directive counseling techniques as those developed by Rogers. As I mentioned before, I think that some psychological knowledge is essential in spiritual direction, but too much reliance on psychological counseling could be a hindrance. It may leave the counselee disturbed and may therefore interfere with his awareness of the Holy Spirit's presence.

Especially in the case of priests and religious it often happens that the underlying problem is a spiritual one, and at times the psychologist does not recognize this or does not know how to deal

18

with it. Sometimes what the counselee needs is a deep awareness of God's loving kindness for him personally. For then the most basic need of a human being is met, namely an acceptance of himself as lovable and an awareness that, even if nobody else were to love him, God certainly does. When he is convinced of this, many of his psychological problems may disappear.

But when these spiritual truths do not satisfy the person, then there is a need for psychological counseling. It often happens that a person who is getting spiritual counseling is also getting psychological counseling at the same time, especially if his problem is not deep-seated. With the consent of the client, I have worked with a psychologist who phones me from time to time to ask what I am doing with this mutual client. He is just as interested in what I am doing for the person as I am in what he is doing. Of course, the client's consent is necessary. Moreover, with a priest or religious, I think the spiritual dimension is extremely important to his psychological makeup. If there is a serious conflict in his spiritual life, it is going to show up psychologically.

One of the more difficult situations arises when there is no serious psychological difficulty but there appear signs of anxiety. How is one to discover what the phenomenon means? I have found that this problem is often solved by the passage of time. When you work with people for a long period of time you discover whether or not their anxiety or guilt is neurotic. If the anxiety or a constant fear or a constant return to this sense of guilt, if, in other words, the sense of well-being is not present, this could be an indication of a wrong choice of vocation. It could also mean an unwillingness to bear the cross imposed by a true vocation. In the latter case there is need to enlighten and to give encouragement.

You will at times be faced with the need to advise a person to go to someone else for spiritual or psychological counseling. When you are giving direction to a certain individual, one of you becomes conscious that «We're just not meeting; one of us is out over his depth here.» If that is the situation, then I think it is time for the counselor in all humility to advise that person to seek somebody else.

Now, in some instances this may be because of the intellectual calibre of the counselee; he may be beyond the counselor. In this case usually what happens is that the person simply stops coming. Because he is not being satisfied with you, he shops around in hope of finding someone else. If you yourself feel uneasy after having worked with a client for quite a while, and you think nothing beneficial is happening, then I believe it is time for him to approach somebody else. In fact, you are responsible for initiating the change.

It may well be that psychological counseling is needed at this time. If this is the case, you have to be careful and delicate. There is a sort of happy balance between your confiding faith in the Holy Spirit and your awareness of being over your depth with some people.

At times it is important for you as a spiritual counselor to indicate to the person when the counseling you are engaged in becomes more psychological in emphasis than spiritual. If I am talking with a person and I say, «What do you think about your relationship with your mother and father?», I usually tell him that while this is more properly a psychological consideration, it has an important bearing on his spiritual life. This is so because one's relationship with God is deeply influenced by the relationship with his father and mother in the first years of life.

Essential to all this work is trust. The person has come to you out of trust. To ask him to go to another counselor might pose a new difficulty for him. In that case, because you have become conscious of problems that you cannot handle yourself, your aim in counseling him should be to help him gain enough freedom to seek further psychological help if it is necessary.

It is sometimes difficult and humiliating to have to tell the counselee that you are unable to help him further with certain problems but that another counselor capable of doing so is available. It may be necessary to assure him that you still love him and that you desire to maintain the friendly relationship you have reached with each other. You should let him know that you will continue to support him but that it would be better for him if he could receive special help from someone else. You really have to make it clear that, even though you are sending him to another counselor, it is because of your own limitations and not for other reasons. In order to be truthful in your love and in your humility somehow you must gently convey to him the fact that only your genuine concern for his welfare has suggested the need for outside help.

In certain situations the counselee may harm his director or be using the director as a crutch. When the counselor realizes that a situation of this kind makes him unable to help his client the sooner he convinces the counselee to go to someone else, the better for both of them. A counselor ought to recognize his own limitations precisely in order that the other can grow in freedom.

A good counselor is one who directs toward independence, and I think that in any counseling relationship you are trying to get your client to stand on his own two feet. Right from the beginning there is a gentle pushing away, combined with support and trust. The relationship necessarily starts with dependency, but real spiritual counseling has to grow in such a way that both stand free while making decisions together in the Lord. In short, when you are relating well with somebody, the trend of the flow is toward a relationship of freedom.

I am convinced that the counselor who is aware of his inadequacies and his own need to be loved will know how to avoid setting up a dependent relationship. When this is unavoidable he must refuse to give counsel. If he is living a satisfactory life elsewhere, enjoying in-depth relationships with some and truly adult friendships with others this danger becomes minimal in counseling. But when the love needs of the counselor himself are unfulfilled outside the counseling field, the situation can be dangerous both for him and for others.

Thus, the counselor should not enter this area lightly. More harm can be done than good. And simply to know and acknowledge one's unsatisfied need for love, or other weakness does not prevent the subtle clues of uneasiness and tension from being sent out to the «other» in such a counseling relationship. Then he is not freeing the counselee, nor is he helping him to grow in the Spirit. Sometimes, consciously or unconsciously, the director may actually foster an attitude of dependency. Then openness and growth are impeded.

Briefly, it is essential to be conscious how easily a counselor's own needs may come to dictate certain attitudes and responses in the counselee. In particular cases we may find ourselves caught in a situation of that sort without being able to escape it. But if the consciousness is there we can at least go to someone else for help to grow in our own freedom.

If I may turn now to a problem in this area that has been much discussed, what exactly is the bearing of a person's psychological weaknesses on his degree of spiritual perfection? How serious does the psychological impairment need to be before it can really prevent one from reaching true spiritual heights? An answer to this question requires some preliminary attention to the words «perfection» and «high degree of perfection.»

In spiritual direction too much emphasis on these

expressions does not help. Each person has his own, unique relationship with God. On the other hand, an objective system of measurement, one that applies equally to everybody, is not easy to find. You cannot really draw a graph showing one person holier than another or locating your counselee on a higher or lower degree of perfection than his neighbor's. For example, in terms of religious «perfection» alone, you might argue that a retarded child could be just as holy as the most intelligent saint. But, in fact, no adequate scale of progress could ever be designed for such comparisons.

The beautiful and consoling truth is that God has created not groups of people who are numerically different, but unique individuals with special qualities, talents and limitations of their own. It is our personal relationship with the Lord that we are concerned with rather than the higher or lower degree of perfection that we reach. Each human person responds with the individual talents and graces that God has given him.

But I agree that at certain times an individual person can become aware that he is more deeply united with Christ than he is at other times, and therefore he can look at his own graph and see himself objectively. This would be a type of Particular Examen in which he focuses not on his acts but on his total attitude. It would seem that, the holier a person gets, the more conscious he is of his dependence on God, the more grateful for God's love, and the more aware of not co-operating with grace. This makes him more humble, as he experiences more love from God.

It is not necessary for a person to have a sound psychological base before he can enjoy a sound spiritual life. I suggested earlier, that some people who are psychologically unwell are, in fact, capable of deep and generous responses to God's spiritual invitations. Moreover, it seems true that even the director could suffer from some limited form of psychological disturbance and still be a good director, precisely because he can then appreciate better the psychic troubles experienced by others.

But it should be stressed that certain compulsive tendencies or inclinations could seriously endanger spiritual direction: if they are not sufficiently controlled in one's behavior, they will easily be projected onto the other. This would depend on the degree of freedom achieved by the director within the emotional realm. Unless he gains enough freedom here, he will only become a further stimulus to neurotic guilt or other troubles in his counselee. I am simply emphasizing the distinction between the psychological and spiritual areas. I think this distinction is important to recognize. A person can be psychologically disturbed, yet be operating fairly well spiritually. Even so, he ought to seek psychological help.

I have maintained that despite certain psychological limitations, a spiritually sound counselor could be helpful to others. But is it possible for the reverse to be true? Can real help come from a psychologically healthy counselor who is not spiritually sound?

If by «spiritually sound» we mean sanctity, then very few people would have the audacity to be counselors. But a person can be a very good, objective judge of other people and be capable of counseling them well without being holy. In fact, I would be suspicious if he thought himself holy. St. Teresa of Avila felt that it was important to consult prudent and learned men in theology even if they were not spiritual and did not practice prayer.

On the other hand, spiritual soundness could mean that the director had good spiritual judgment, especially with respect to himself. I would say that, if he is unable to judge what is going on in his own spiritual life, he would not be a good judge for others. But good judgment is different from what is meant by holiness. Of course, if he is an out-and-out reprobate, he will not be interested at all in the spiritual. The merely sensual man cannot relish, does not understand, the things of the Spirit. (*cf.* 1 Co 2:14)

The Holy Spirit is a free flowing spirit. We must both submit to his impulse and recognize the direction of his movement. The Spiritual Exercises are the attempt of a great saint to let the Spirit move freely and to recognize that movement in those who experience prayer. Their enduring value is evident in their effect on those who make them today and in the approval of the Church down the centuries.

Through these Exercises the retreatant experiences his creaturehood, his sinfulness, the mercy of God, the call of Christ, and the different demands implicit in that call. He is led to face suffering with Christ, to enjoy glory with Christ, to seek and find Christ — all the spiritual realities given to those who believe in him.

Even outside the context of the Exercises, it is important for you in directing another to identify the particular kind of experience he is undergoing at the time. If he seems unaware of any such experience, your presence and counsel is needed to enlighten him about his condition. The apparent absence of spiritual development in his life may itself be a form of «desert» experience, or it may indicate a willful barrier to grace. After identifying the counselee's condition, you should try to understand its significance for this individual person. But paramount in your awareness at every stage (and this again separates the spiritual from the psychological counselor) must be your conviction that any growth whatever is entirely dependent on the grace of God.

An article by John Harriott in *The Way* (October, 1970) has much to say on this essential dependence on grace. It is called «Himself He Cannot Save.»[3] In this article Harriott, after distinguishing the biological, psychological and spiritual aspects

25

of human life reminds us of the great remarkable contribution that medical and other sciences have made in controlling the biological component of our lives. This has gone so far, he notes, that man can substantially influence his own biological development up to the actual moment of death. Even on the point of death, medical science can keep the heart beating for days or weeks or months.

Harriott then goes on to consider the psychological dimension and the ways, that new understanding in this area can bring a large measure of assistance to personal growth. But he also stresses the situations and aspects of life that are beyond human control whether by medical or psychological means. Death is one of these moments when «himself he cannot save.» The awareness of approaching death can undercut every one of man's activities. Salvation is beyond him.

Of course, the human predicament is more general than the mere thought of death might suggest. At several points in the Exercises St. Ignatius brings man face to face with his helplessness and his need of others. As the exercitant progresses through the Exercises, he becomes conscious that he cannot save himself. This is usually one of his earliest and most basic insights: «I cannot save myself: I need a savior.» Although other experiences precede and follow, precisely here we become actually conscious of the spiritual depths of our being. This admission, «I need a savior,» is the fundamental Christian ascetical principle. Many of us have been given a kind of ascetical training, intentionally or otherwise, which schools us to think that we can pick ourselves up by our bootstraps, that we can save ourselves in the spiritual realm as well as in the biological and psychological realms. But we cannot save ourselves. This, then, becomes one of the important ascetical principles of spiritual counseling.

Thus, at some point in spiritual counseling you must face the question; «Does this person think he can save himself or not?» If, like many today he silently assumes he can save himself, then he needs to be enlightened on basic truths of the faith. Keeping in mind the directives of Ignatius, [22] he needs to reflect prayerfully on himself and on all his relationships.

Moreover, even if he has an intellectual grasp of the fact that he cannot save himself, he may continue to behave in practice as if he could save himself and to feel emotionally that he must save himself. When this divergence has been detected a wise counselor will try to move him from a merely intellectual awareness to a fully personal acceptance of what he knows.

In this endeavor the counselor must hold to the truth that this is God's work and that he himself is only God's instrument. In presenting to the client man's need for salvation as a topic for prayer, the counselor is himself aware that only God's grace can bring a person to a deep awareness, in the totality of his personhood, that he cannot save himself.

In problems of this sort the remarkable complexity of human nature becomes apparent, as does the complexity of spiritual counseling. Man is not just body and soul, intellect and will, but spirit as well. And all of these are united in a single person — in perplexing confusion. It is only too easy for him to assent intellectually to a proposition without making a total submission of himself to the truth. It is hard to commit oneself fully to another person, even to the person of God the Father or to Jesus Christ, who is Truth itself.

Spiritual direction differs from psychological counseling in both context and content. The director and his client are not alone but surrounded by the love of the Trinity. They are not to listen only to each other but also to the Spirit speaking in each of them. Since both must be believing and praying persons both share in the life of the same Spirit. The aim of such counseling is not so much to make the counselee independent or free in himself, but rather to live in freedom with the Spirit who lives in him and in all believing persons.

CHAPTER 1

PURPOSE OF THE SPIRITUAL EXERCISES

*Then he said to his disciples, «That is why I am telling you
not to worry about your life and what you are to eat, nor
about your body and how you are to clothe it. For life
means more than food, and the body more than clothing.
Think of the ravens. They do not sow or reap; they have
no storehouses and no barns; yet God feeds them. And
how much more are you worth than the birds! Can any of
you, for all his worrying, add a single cubit to his span of
life? If the smallest things, therefore, are outside your
control, why worry about the rest? Think of the flowers;
they never have to spin or weave; yet, I assure you, not
even Solomon in all his regalia was robed like one of
these. Now if that is how God clothes the grass in the field
which is there today and thrown into the furnace
tomorrow, how much more will he look after you, you
men of little faith! But you, you must not set your hearts
on things to eat and things to drink; nor must you worry.
It is the pagans of this world who set their hearts on all
these things. Your Father well knows you need them. No;
set your hearts on his kingdom, and these other things will
be given you as well.*

*«There is no need to be afraid, little flock, for it has
pleased your Father to give you the kingdom.» (Lk 12:22-
32)*

I think you know there is some difference of opinion
about the purpose of the Spiritual Exercises of St. Ignatius
Loyola. Ignatius speaks of them as «Spiritual Exercises which

have as their purpose the conquest of self and the regulation of one's life in such a way that no decision is made under the influence of any inordinate attachment.» [21]

This proposition of Ignatius would seem to say — and this is the view of most commentators — that the purpose of the Exercises is for the exercitant to arrive at some kind of a decision. But other commentators have suggested that the Exercises are meant to be a school of prayer or an instrument for bringing one into union with God.

It is also possible that these two expressions of the purpose of the Exercises come to the same thing. Maybe the difference is only semantic. Whether one is making a decision or achieving closer union with God, it would seem that a more reliable decision demands closer union with God and that the closer one draws to God, the more often and the more stringently does God demand of him decisions in response.

I think that the key to both approaches to the Exercises is the need of a person to become free. The Exercises are an instrument to help the person come to freedom. The freedom I am speaking about here is a kind of realized, existential freedom, freedom with oneself and freedom within oneself. It is what might be called ultimate freedom, the freedom that accompanies the deep awareness of the ultimate meaning of one's life.

This freedom requires an acceptance of oneself historically as coming from God and going to God and being with God. It includes a sense of well being, of self-identity, of basic peace. One who is thus free can in peace answer the questions, «Who am I?», «Where am I going?» Thus, the questions Ignatius poses, «What have I done for Christ? What am I doing for Christ? What ought I to do for Christ?», form part of the process of freedom and are its expression.

The special level of freedom intended here results from the

action of the Spirit in us: «this hope is not deceptive, because the love of God has been poured into our hearts by the Holy Spirit which has been given us.» (Rm 5:5) Spiritual Exercises sharpen our awareness of this love and of the Spirit's presence making us free.

When Ignatius speaks of «Spiritual Exercises which have as their purpose the conquest of self and the regulation of one's life,» [21] one may think that the author is a pelagian. The word «pelagian,» derives from the name of Pelagius, a monk who lived around 400 A.D. He taught that man could save himself by good works. The Church condemned this teaching as heretical, insisting that God's grace is the impetus of every good work and that the grace of baptism is necessary for salvation.

Nevertheless, after the condemnation a group of Pelagius's followers began to teach that, although man needs the grace of baptism, thereafter he is capable of saving himself. This modified teaching was called «semi-pelagianism,» and it was likewise condemned. Any good action that is instrumental for salvation is made in response to a grace from God and is carried out with that grace. Even the impetus to co-operate with grace is itself a grace. And yet it is man's free act. The problem, then, is the place of free choice in all of this grace-filled activity.

The exercitant might think that he is going to conquer himself, that by his own efforts he will succeed in regulating his life in such a way that no decision is made under the influence of any inordinate attachment. But we know that these are «spiritual» exercises and not psychological therapy. Ignatius takes it for granted that God's grace is always operating.

Serious study of this supposition by Ignatius could open up a discussion on the theological question of grace in its whole scope, that is, Father and Son and Spirit giving themselves interiorly to us to free us and raise us to their love.

Everyone moved by the Spirit is a son of God. The spirit you received is not the spirit of slaves bringing fear into your lives again; it is the spirit of sons, and it makes us cry out. «Abba, Father!» The Spirit himself and our spirit bear united witness that we are children of God. And if we are children we are heirs as well: heirs of God and co-heirs with Christ, sharing his sufferings so as to share his glory. (Rm 8:14-17)

I would prefer, instead, to concentrate on the question of inordinate attachments. Many people think that all attachments are inordinate, but they are not. There are some attachments that are ordinate, well ordered to the end for which we are created. They bring one closer to God and to other people. The problem is not with the latter; it is with inordinate attachments.

The inordinate attachments are those that turn one in on oneself, that are strictly concerned with self. They are self-centered and selfish. Ignatius speaks, then, about such attachments as inordinate because these attachments are enslaving. They are the ones that chain the person and prevent him from being free with himself, free with other human beings and free in the whole context of life.

Let me, therefore, say this about the purpose of the Exercises: whether they are an instrument to bring one into union with God or to make a decision, the Exercises are intended to bring one into a position of freedom with respect to himself, with respect to other human beings and with respect to God. It is in this context that the Holy Spirit can make himself known.

Someone has said that the problem of knowing the will of God is not the big problem. The big problem is freedom, indifference, detachment. When I use the word, «indifference,» I am not using it in the sense that one is to be indifferent to people. Nor does the word «detached» mean that one is to be a detached, unfeeling, unresponsive person. We are speaking here about the freedom that a person has within himself in relation to everything else that is not God. It means to be dominated by Jesus Christ.

This is the basic freedom we are hoping to obtain in the Exercises. In fact it is an experience of grace. Once a person has this kind of freedom, then the will of God is probably very clear to him. If there is this freedom, often there is given with it the strength from God to do his will. So the freedom we are seeking is the difficult thing to accept from God, and that is the conquest of self that Ignatius outlines for us, but always in the context of grace.

It is here that we find the reason for doing the Exercises before reading them. As pelagian as Ignatius may sound at the beginning, by the time you arrive at the «Contemplation to Attain Love of God» you know that the entire thirty days are lived in the context of faith and love and acceptance of «gift.» The whole process of «conquering» oneself is accomplished by the working of the Spirit dwelling in us. The action of the Spirit is expressed in the graces one prays for in the course of the Exercises: the grace of sorrow, the grace of being chosen under the standard of Christ, and the other specific graces. This is clear evidence that, despite appearances, the method of the Exercises is not pelagian.

Freedom, then, is one of the fundamental graces of the Spiritual Exercises, and it leads to the making of an election and to union with God. Of course, other important benefits may result from the Exercises, for example, an appreciation of the cosmic Christ, which comes with the third and fourth weeks and the «Contemplation to Attain Love of God.» But the most important process is the attainment of this freedom — the freedom of the sons of God. It can only be known by experience. And we experience it as a grace from God by living consciously in the sphere of the Trinity. Along with the experience itself comes the certainty that it is a grace and that it is the work of the Spirit.

Since the attainment in some degree of the freedom described here is, I believe, the purpose of the Exercises as a whole, it follows that anyone who directs another through the thirty days of prayer should keep it in mind at every stage. But how should a spiritual director, engaged with a client outside the time of retreat, put this principle to work in his counseling?

It is frequent enough to discover a serious lack of freedom in a counselee. When there are grounds for suspecting the presence of such a block to spiritual growth, the director ought first of all to identify, if he can, the actual cause of the «unfreedom.» Is it a distorted image of God? a secret sin? an inordinate attachment to some object or position or person?

Once the cause has been discovered, the client should be given prayer material that will help him with his particular difficulty. At various places in the chapters that follow, both the causes of unfreedom and the kinds of prayer material that are helpful will be discussed. It should be noted, however, that often enough a deep, inordinate attachment cannot be overcome outside a thirty-day retreat. In that case the director should perhaps try to prepare his counselee to undertake the full Spiritual Exercises.

CHAPTER 2

THE PRINCIPLE AND FOUNDATION

Moses was looking after the flock of Jethro, his father-in-law, priest of Midian. He led his flock to the far side of the wilderness and came to Horeb, the mountain of God. There the angel of Yahweh appeared to him in the shape of a flame of fire, coming from the middle of a bush. Moses looked; there was the bush blazing but it was not being burnt up. 'I must go and look at this strange sight,' Moses said 'and see why the bush is not burnt.' Now Yahweh saw him go forward to look, and God called to him from the middle of the bush. 'Moses, Moses!' he said. 'Here I am' he answered. 'Come no nearer' he said. 'Take off your shoes, for the place on which you stand is holy ground. I am the God of your father,' he said 'the God of Abraham, the God of Isaac and the God of Jacob.' At this Moses covered his face, afraid to look at God. (Ex 3: 1-6)

At this point I begin to enter into the text of the *Exercises* in order to consider in each of the major sections the basic ascetical principles that are involved. As I hope to make clear, these principles are important for anyone who directs another in prayer or who gives spiritual counsel outside the time of retreat.

The «Principle and Foundation» opens with a definite affirmation of human creaturehood: «Man has been created to praise, reverence, and serve our Lord God, and by this means to save his soul.» Now, Louis Evely maintains that these words contain heresy. He feels that this kind of statement gives a false image of God. God did not create man, says Evely, in order to obtain praise, reverence and service but to share his divine love. And we must agree with the final phrase: man is certainly an expression of God's infinite love.

But Ignatius's statement is not heresy. For we are the recipients of this love. We experience God's love in our very being, and, as a result of this experience, we become aware of the need to praise, reverence and serve him. In this way we actually express our innermost meaning as persons who respond to the love of God. Evely, however, is rightly concerned with false images of God. Many people have, in fact, an image of God as Santa Claus or as a policeman, and this faulty image influences their approach to prayer and their attitude to this world. If Ignatius's statement about man's creation is read in that way, then Evely's criticism is warranted.

It is therefore important to consider the «Principle and Foundation» as composed, not from the standpoint of a God who makes strict demands upon man, but from the standpoint of man's own experience, of man's sense of total dependence on God. It then becomes clear that Ignatius is talking about creaturehood, about the human experience of being a creature.

«Man is created to praise, reverence and serve God our Lord, and by this means to save his soul.» [23] Only man is free to praise, reverence and serve God, and only in this free action does he truly become man, possess his own being, and save his soul. «To save his soul» is a phrase that needs to be understood. We would say, «to save himself.» (At the same time, it must be stressed, all this is the work of the Lord.) By giving himself to this purpose, man is able to find a meaning for his existence. Today we might rather say that saving one's soul is the equivalent of

36

making oneself meaningful, becoming meaningful to oneself.

The animals and the other things on the face of the earth are a sort of mute witness in their innocence, but man is a being that can look to the future. There is a future horizon for all of us. It is in view of that horizon that our freedom is found. We are aware of possible actions in front of us, and we have a free choice to make concerning this future although the choice is in the «now.» Only man is free to praise, reverence, and serve God in this freedom.

The phrase, «to save his own soul,» also suggests the need to distinguish between the love of self and selfishness or self-centeredness. It is right, after all, for man to love himself. He is a being of love. And he truly loves himself when he accepts himself and when he accepts the «Yes» of his destiny, the goal of life's journey.

When he accepts the pull of the Spirit and says «Yes» to that, he finds meaning, he loves himself, and he reaches his fulfillment. I think it is Karl Rahner who remarked that man understands himself as meaningful when he experiences God filling up his emptiness. It is important, therefore, to realize that this phrase, «to save his own soul,» in the *Exercises* means to find fulfillment, to come to meaningfulness in himself, in the totality of his being.

I had an experience recently in which I was face-to-face with creaturehood. Not my own creaturehood, but that of someone else. But I felt its impact. I was driving back from Toronto and, about two miles the other side of Milton, there was an accident. I am not sure what happened. It was such a mess; I was quite upset. I believe the people involved were driving a Maverick; at any rate, one of those small new cars. It would appear that either the driver turned in front of a big truck and the truck was going too fast and smashed into him, or that the driver of the little car had to put on the brakes too quickly, or something else. Whatever the cause, it happened. The small car looked as if a big sledgehammer had hit it, and its three occupants were flung out. The mother's body was lying far away beside a fence, and the father was about fifteen feet off the road. The little child, about four years old, was still alive. Someone who had gotten there ahead of me was holding the little child in his arms. How the child survived is hard to say.

The whole situation expressed the helpless weakness of humanity. Creaturehood was staring me in the face: the unconcern of the child, the tenderness of the man holding him, the motionless bodies of the parents, the crumpled, smoking machinery, dust hanging in the air. Somehow, despite my confusion, the pathetic scene called forth my deepest religious feelings.

To come upon a fatal accident is perhaps a rather negative way of approaching the sense of creaturehood that underlies the «Principle and Foundation.» Of course, in the *Exercises* creaturehood is presented differently — not only from the angle of sin and death, but mainly from the angle of love. For we are beings of love, created out of love. Thus, before a person actually starts the Exercises and encounters some of the other important ascetical experiences, he must begin with the awareness that he is a creature, but a creature of love. During the retreat many directors start a retreatant off reading passages from scripture such as Hosea 11, Isaiah 43, Isaiah 49, Ephesians 1 and 3, Psalms 8 and 139. By praying over these passages, he may come to experience himself more deeply as a being of love, totally dependent on the Lord and on his love.

One of the important experiences of the person you are directing is this deep awareness. He is a creature totally dependent on God, who has brought him into being and who keeps him in existence. He is something like the little flame on the top of a candle, full of joy and light, yet fragile, easy to blow out, held in existence by an all-loving God.

38

This is an extremely important ascetical position before God. It is basic. You cannot make progress in spiritual direction if your client has not yet experienced his creaturehood. True, you can talk to him about love and try to motivate him in terms of human love. By this means, perhaps, you may gradually get him to recognize that he is a being of love. But the really deep awareness is spiritual. It is the sense of total dependence on a loving God. It is what impelled St. Augustine to say: «I tremble in fear and burn with love.» It is similar to the feeling of the bride going into the bridal chamber: filled with love, yet trembling from a sense of frailty. Such is the sense of creaturehood, a sense of weakness and dependence but security in the face of love.

Now, how do you bring this feeling about? You do not; that is the work of the Spirit. But you can give the person matter to pray over. You can give him such passages as those I mentioned before — Hosea 11, and the others. The sense of creaturehood is not just an intellectual realization. It is not the answer to the catechism question, «Why did God create me?» It is a deep awareness. In some ways it comes from our human condition, and in some ways it comes from grace. It contains a mixture of feelings. It involves a feeling of fear, but at the same time a feeling of security. The Christian knows himself as a dependent being but one surrounded by love. At least, the Christian should be sure that he is safe in the arms of his Creator.

The experience is prior, as far as I am concerned, to indifference or detachment or freedom. You cannot ask a person to be indifferent or detached until he has some awareness of God's love within him. Therefore, when you are giving spiritual direction, this is one of the first goals you hope to achieve. You may do it by getting him to recall experiences he has had of love. In one way or another you try to lead him to be relaxed in God's love for him. Once that is assured, you can start talking to him about freedom or detachment or indifference. And you can start talking about commitment.

Now, interestingly enough, in the «Principle and Foundation» you find these three basic movements: creaturehood, indifference, commitment. It begins with the consideration of creaturehood: «Man is created to praise, reverence, and serve God our Lord, and by this means to save his soul.» [23] The implications of creaturehood are traced in the sub-human realm: «The other things on the face of the earth are created for man to help him in attaining the end for which he is created.»[23] Moreover, «praise, reverence and service» are expressions of total dependence. If anything, the reference to indifference is more explicit: «we must make ourselves indifferent to all created things, as far as we are allowed free choice and are not under any prohibition.»[23] Ignatius says that man must be «indifferent» even to those realities that are most intimate to his being and to his biological and psychological life: «we should not prefer health to sickness, riches to poverty, honor to dishonor, a long life to a short life.»[23] Finally, the exercitant is to go beyond passive indifference and acceptance; he has to see the value of commitment: «Our one desire and choice should be what is more conducive to the end for which we are created.» [23] But the retreatant does not experience creaturehood, indifference, and commitment merely by reading about them. The truth of the «Principle and Foundation» is realized only after one has given himself to unremitting prayer and after he has been endowed with God's grace. This reality is a living thing which may make itself felt only at the end of the thirty days of the Exercises.

Someone asked me the question, «Why, don't we start with the «Contemplation to Attain Love of God»?» Well, in a way, we do that if at the beginning we propose a good deal of scripture on God's love. This could be done before the person is asked to consider indifference and the choice of the «better thing.»

But I think there is a difference between the «Principle and Foundation» and the «Contemplation to Attain Love of God.» The difference is found in the context in which the person is praying. In the «Principle and Foundation,» God is seen as transcendent; man is his creature. The Creator-creature relationship is stressed in terms of reverence, praise and awe. In the «Contemplation to Attain Love of God,» however, I think that there is a greater awareness of the immanence of God. There is a more familiar tone and context. God is right there with his arms around his creature; God is within him because it is the Spirit within him that is urging him on.

At the beginning of spiritual direction, then, you hope that the person will come to you fully aware that he is a being who is loved and loved greatly. If he does not have this awareness because of unfortunate early experiences in the home or because of other circumstances, then as counselor you have to do two things. First, you must love him yourself. At the same time, you dispose yourself to be the instrument by which the Spirit within him will make him aware that he is loved by God. (*cf.* Rm 8:26-27; 1 Jn 4:10) Once he knows that, then perhaps you can start helping him to gain that existential freedom that is necessary for him to live the full Christian life.

What makes man is the love affair. Man is humble when he is overtaken by love. What we are concerned about through the Exercises and in spiritual counseling are the great experiences of life: freedom, encounters with other people, love, death, all these and more, developed through the inner workings of the Spirit in man himself. Being is entrusted to man as a challenge, a summons. He is involved in change, in possibilities of greater being. He is always moving toward the future. He must fully become what he is, that is, a human being. To become a full human being requires the freedom of which we have spoken. Of course, it is an ongoing process in which he is constantly discovering his freedom and becoming aware of new dimensions of unfreedom within himself. As a result, he is sorry for the past and has great hope for the future. It is in the exercise of freedom that man becomes free. The interior awareness is exercised in relation to our own being, to other things, and to other persons. It is the Holy Spirit (Christ's Spirit) freeing man in these relationships.

The particular degree of freedom enjoyed by a person would be a point from which to determine whether this person has a psychological problem. If you can discover what has made the person unfree, that may indicate whether the unfreedom has psychological or spiritual origins. It is possible, of course, that the person might be psychologically unfree but spiritually free. There are certain people who know themselves psychologically and accept themselves psychologically as unfree, yet enjoy a spiritual freedom with it all. It is a beautiful thing when you see it. It is very hard on the person himself because he is tied up in himself, and he knows he is tied up. Yet his relationship with God is good for he knows he is accepted by God.

Perhaps the true meaning of freedom comes home to the retreatant when he applies the «Rules for the Discernment of Spirits» provided towards the end of the *Spiritual Exercises*. Whether a man is experiencing anxiety, or fear, or lack of quiet, or constant temptation, what is in question is his freedom. It may be slavery that he is feeling instead of freedom. To discover this is a great part of the process of discernment. Hopefully he will continue to grow in his grace-filled freedom. But a word of caution is needed. There is a real danger, in making the Exercises and in engaging in any other prayer experience, that he may think at the end of them. «I've got it made.»

It is also true that freedom, whether psychological or

spiritual, is a growing thing, such that every experience is free in a way which maybe you have never known before. You can recognize a lot of unfreedom precisely because of wholly new experiences of freedom; you see much more than ever before.

It is somewhat the same with the saints who consider themselves great sinners. As they advanced, they recognized their unfreedom in a way they never had before. It is possible that one may continue to be aware that he is loved even though he is experiencing some other unfreedoms at the same time. He accepts his own humanity, his creaturehood, even his sinfulness, at the same time that he is hoping and striving to cooperate with the grace of God. He stays open to the urgings of the Spirit who helps him to overcome his unfreedoms. In the case of the saints, grace and sin were seen not as material things but as their personal experience of accepting or rejecting the love of the Father and the Son and the Spirit.

Now, while many great saints experienced themselves as the greatest sinners, some like St. Therese of Lisieux, the little Flower, experienced themselves as little, and not even great as sinners. I think the example of the Little Flower tends to emphasize that humility is the important thing and not the boasting about being a great sinner. Therese of Lisieux thought of herself as a little child, as a dependent being, as a being of love totally dependent on the Lord; and she was probably very much aware of her creaturehood. Although aware of her inconsistency and her faults, she was not going to let these interfere with the relationship she had with the Father.

In keeping with this attitude, theology maintains that redemption is a purely gratuitous act on the part of God. No sin of man calls for Jesus's death on the cross. This action of the Trinity can only be explained as the supreme act of love on the part of the Trinity to bring man back to fulfillment, to bring him into union with the Trinity and make man at-one with God by the at-one-ment of the Paschal Mystery.

I think the other saints had realized this, but they expressed it differently. When they felt themselves to be the greatest of sinners, I think all they meant was that their experience of grace was immeasurably more than their own meager response to grace. It was not that they felt they were going to hell. Rather, they were totally conscious of love, and they felt that they were not co-operating fully with it.

Basically, then, I cannot see a contradiction here. In both instances there is the experience of being loved by God. Therese expressed this experience in one way; other saints express it in another way. The intensity of the experience of love is, of course, a great grace. It cannot be obtained by a man's human effort.

Thus, the Exercises begin with a consideration and awareness of creaturehood. The retreatant becomes aware of the mystery of his existence. More than that, he knows himself as a dependent being, but a dependent being of love. Such an awareness, arising out of the Spirit-filled context of prayer, brings with it awe and freedom and desire to serve. It begins within him the process of knowing that he is loved for himself and not for what he does. He is a being of love, as small as he is, even in his sins. He experiences the desire to praise and serve God. But how can this be achieved? I will take this up in the next chapter.

CHAPTER 3

FREEDOM AND COMMITMENT

Now some of John's disciples had opened a discussion with a Jew about purification, so they went to John and said, «Rabbi, the man who was with you on the far side of the Jordan, the man to whom you bore witness, is baptizing now; everyone is going to him.» And John replied: «A man can lay claim only to what is given him from heaven. You yourselves can bear me out: I said I myself am not the Christ; I am the one who has been sent in front of him. The bride is only for the bridegroom; and yet the bridegroom's friend, who stands there and listens, is glad when he hears the bridegroom's voice. This same joy I feel, and now it is complete. He must grow greater, I must grow smaller. He who comes from above is above all others; he who is born of the earth is earthly himself and speaks in an earthly way. He who comes from Heaven bears witness to the things he has seen and heard, even if his testimony is not accepted; though all who do accept his testimony are attesting the truthfulness of God, since he whom God has sent speaks God's own words: God gives him the Spirit without reserve. The Father loves the Son and has entrusted everything to him. Anyone who believes in the Son has eternal life, but anyone who refuses to believe in the Son will never see life: the anger of God stays on him.» (Jn 3:25-36)

The «Principle and Foundation» continues: «The other things on the face of the earth are created for man to help him in attaining the end for which he is created.»[23] And everyone nods his head and says, «That's right.» But he must read the next sentence as well: «Hence, man is to make use of them in as far as they help him in the attainment of his end, and he must rid himself of them in as far as they prove a hindrance to him.» [23] Then the questions start to come! How can this be done? How is a man going to use creatures correctly? There is only too much evidence of our failure in this. Are we to say, then, that the end-product of the «Principle and Foundation» is confusion of mind and a quiet despair? We have long since experienced our inability to use creatures correctly, to truly serve the Lord.

For the moment, Ignatius gives no answer. He merely notes that a man must make himself indifferent to all created things: «Consequently, as far as we are concerned, we should not prefer health to sickness, riches to poverty, honor to dishonor, a long life to a short life... Our one desire and choice should be what is more conducive to the end for which we are created.»[23] Now this end is to choose what is more for the praise, reverence and service of God and the salvation of one's soul.

This is the difficult thing, to commit oneself to doing what is more for God's greater honor and glory. The Exercises in a sense are designed to bring a person to make such a commitment, but in the rest of the Exercises, as well as in the «Principle and Foundation» he discovers that no explicitly formulated answer is given. As he works his way through the Exercises, he finds no set of rules telling him exactly what the will of God is for him personally. All that is given is prayer material. As he works his way through it he may gradually dispose himself to gain freedom.

What is to be done, what is to be chosen, will be discovered as he grows in his capacity to act and to choose. As a result, he finds that he is not making a choice after all. What is really happening is

46

that the Lord is disposing, constantly disposing him. The desire to do the *magis,* the more, the greater thing, demands freedom and indifference. That is the difficult thing, to come to freedom, to indifference.

Ignatius's description of indifference is that of a «balance at equilibrium, without leaning to either side.» [179, *cf.* 15] One of the confusing things about indifference and detachment is that most people have looked upon them as negative. Moreover, one of the instructions that Ignatius gives in annotation 16 also looks extremely negative:

> Hence, that the Creator and Lord may work with greater certainty in His creature, if the soul chance to be inordinately attached or inclined to anything, it is very proper that it rouse itself by the exertion of all its powers to desire the opposite of that to which it is wrongly attached. Thus if one's attachment leads him to seek and to hold an office or a benefice, not for the honor and glory of God our Lord, nor for the spiritual welfare of souls, but for his own personal gain and temporal interests, he should strive to rouse a desire for the contrary. Let him be insistent in prayer and in his other spiritual exercises in begging God for the reverse, that is, that he neither seek such office or benefice, nor anything else, unless the Divine Majesty duly regulate his desires and change his former attachment. As a result, the reason he wants or retains anything will be solely the service, honor, and glory of the Divine Majesty. [16]

Now this should recall to your minds the note of the «Three Classes of Men.» [157] As Ignatius presents it, it is negative. He is saying that, if a person has an inordinate attachment to something, he should beg our Lord to give him the opposite inclination and even to take the object away.

Yes, indifference has a negative aspect to it, but the basic thrust of indifference and detachment is beyond the negative. It is not so much leaving all things as finding a person, the person of Jesus Christ. It means being so dominated by love for Christ (which is actually Christ's love for him) that he is free of all else. He wishes to be and do what God wants him to be and do. It leads him to desire the will of God so strongly that he wishes to choose the better way of praising, reverencing and serving God.

Freedom moves to commitment, but that commitment proves in turn to be a new freedom. A man can be free with respect to all other things only if he is dominated by God. And so this indifference that Ignatius is speaking about comes only with an awareness of God's love and a consciousness of his goodness.

Now, what Ignatius is speaking about is exemplified in the attitude of Abraham towards the sacrifice of his son; the attitude of our Lady expressed in her *fiat,* «be it done unto me according to thy word»;   the attitude of John the Baptist expressed in his words, «He must increase, I must decrease.» Abraham went up the mountain for three days with Isaac. He was so dominated by God, so filled with faith and trust in God, that he could stand indifferent to all other created things. Abraham's indifference did not mean that he did not suffer nor that he did not love Isaac. But he had gained a freedom that enabled him to trust God to the extreme.

Ignatius gives examples of this attitude at the very beginning of the *Exercises,* warning us that we should not prefer «health to sickness, riches to poverty, honor to dishonor, a long life to a short life.» These pairings represent existential aspects of man in that they pertain to his basic drives and desires. Health and sickness are related to the desire for life; riches and poverty, to the desire to be accepted; and, finally, a long life and a short life, to the desire for survival. Ignatius asks the exercitant to consider indifference in terms of these basic needs of his being.

48

But this kind of indifference is not obtained until twenty or thirty days of the retreat have passed.

Karl Rahner has this to say on indifference:

> Nor is indifference the mere resolution not to let oneself be carried along by the crowd; it demands, rather, the existential distance from things that is self-appropriated in such a way that it even frees the will to reject its own previous prejudices. Even the attitude of accepting everything that happens in silence — which in itself is very difficult — is less than what is demanded here. The *Spiritual Exercises* propose an active indifference in virtue of which we are to act in such a way that both the using and the leaving of things can and must be our own responsibility. ... This distance from things is a goal that must always be re-won again and again.[4]

Indifference is valuable not for its own sake but for the choice of what is more conducive to some end. A man's aim in choosing is to conform himself freely and entirely to what God chooses. Indifference appears as a crucial element in man's freedom, the freedom which he does not desire to wrest to himself alone, but to leave open to God's loving intimations. And Rahner also warns: «Unless we operate on a principle of indifference and the *magis* there is danger in life of self-centeredness, a danger of going from one excess to another.» He gives as examples the over-emphasis on the law in Pharisaism and on autonomy of conscience in paganism, where there is no law from God.

The concept of indifference is as important to understand as the reality is difficult to live. Ignatius says we should not prefer a «long life to a short life.» Although most might like to have a long life, there might be some who would like to have a short life. A man is to be indifferent to either. There might be some who would prefer sickness to health; it is a little easier lying in bed all the time than working. Some would prefer poverty to riches because riches entail responsibility, as seen in the «Three Classes of Men.» Some like dishonor more than honor. You never know; the choice can go either way.

It is said that, when Francis Xavier first went to Japan, he wore an old cassock which had seen years of hard use. It was all frayed and tattered, a perfect witness to indifference for the western mind. But, when he appeared wearing it in the Japanese court, he became the object of scornful laughter. This in itself would not have worried Xavier but for its effect on his mission. So the next time he came to court, he was clad in all the regalia of an ambassador and had an appropriate retinue. For he realized that a certain amount of display would be for the greater honor and glory of God. If this was the way he would be heard, then he was willing to enter in the guise of a man of wealth and position. Indifference implies flexibility; it is important to grasp the significance of the phrase, «we should not prefer.»

Indifference and openness before God are necessary for the constant dialogue of prayer. The demands of God are countered by man's responsibility. In his dialogue with God a man is really trying to understand his relationship with God, but prior to the dialogue is the need to be open. He wants what God wants, but he is not sure what God wants. Consider Job; he insisted that he was a just man. He could not understand his predicament; and he kept badgering God for an explanation. Yet we know from his own words that he was a free man, an indifferent man: «Naked I came from my mother's womb, naked I shall return. Yahweh gave, Yahweh has taken back. Blessed be the name of Yahweh!» (Jb 1:21)

Job had this fundamental freedom before God, but it did not

prevent him from arguing with God. Jeremiah and Moses, too, had this basic indifference at the same time that they were arguing with God. I do not think there is conflict here. It simply means that these men were very conscious of their responsibility. What we are discussing now belongs to the difficult realm of grace and responsibility and freedom. It is very hard to understand this mystery in which man is free and responsible while God is doing everything.

In understanding the «Principle and Foundation,» it is important to distinguish between persons and things. A man cannot be indifferent to persons. But there is a very fine distinction here. He is commanded to love persons, and, in that sense, he can have an ordinate attachment to persons. But the real question in such an attachment arises: «Am I in love with the person, or am I attached to and in love with the thing I call a person?»

I think the Abraham story is to the point here. Kierkegaard has a beautiful commentary on Abraham and Isaac in *Fear and Trembling*. This magnificent piece of work interprets what goes on inside Abraham as he receives a command from the Lord to go and kill his son. Kierkegaard describes the anguish and discernment that goes on in the mind of Abraham. I would say that Abraham loved Isaac, truly loved him. He was rightly attached to his son. That is what made the task of going up the mountain so difficult. And so there was indifference in this relationship. What I think happened is that, as Abraham went up the mountain, his inordinate attachment to Isaac gradually disappeared. There was a purifying process going on.

In other words, his relationship to Isaac was this: Isaac was a person and Isaac was his son and so he loved Isaac as a person and as his son. But Isaac was also the means by which his name would be carried down through the centuries. Now, Abraham had to become aware of that distinction; and he had to continue to love and be ordinately attached to Isaac the person and Isaac the son, but he had to become purified of his inordinate attachment to Isaac as progenitor of the race. I think this is what God did with Abraham as he went up the mountain; he purified him of that inordinate attachment. There are ordinate attachments to persons and there are inordinate attachments to persons. Basically, the indifference of the «Principle and Foundation» concerns a man's relationships to non-persons.

Is it possible to say that, along with the promise of Isaac's carrying on the race, God also gave Abraham unbreakable trust that God could fulfill his promise and still ask of Abraham the sacrifice of his son? There is a famous text in the *Letter to the Hebrews* to the effect that Abraham believed God could even raise the dead. (Heb 11:19) Abraham's experience of God's goodness and God's strength and God's wisdom was such that he could trust God.

And yet, the Lord has some very strong language on this matter. He says in one place, «Unless a man hates father, mother, brother, and sister for my sake he cannot be my disciple.» What is he saying to us in this powerful statement? He is saying, «If you want to be my disciple, you have to be dominated by me. I have to be the total person in your life, to the extent that you may even appear to hate your father, mother, brother and sister. You have to undergo that criticism.» He cannot mean that a true Christian must hate his father and mother. Too many of his other statements disavow that notion. He even says that «God loves the sinner.» And he commands men to be like their heavenly Father, who loves sinners. So obviously we ought to love our parents. Thus, I think we have to make the kind of distinction given above in the Abraham story.

This freedom that comes with indifference is extremely dependent on one's faith in another person. It is like the father who takes his little boy to the dentist. If the father did not go with the little boy, you would never find the boy in that dentist's chair. Yet, because he trusts his father, he is willing to go through some degree of suffering. That is why I said earlier that, practically speaking, a retreatant has to have the «Contemplation to Attain Love of God» in some form or another before he even starts the «Principle and Foundation.» Maybe there should be at the beginning of the Exercises three days of prayer on God's love for man. Only with faith in God can we be detached or indifferent because by indifference the person surrenders totally to God as Mary did. Sometimes one can surrender intellectually to another's argument but not surrender personally to that other. Is such a man unsure of himself in his faith because he feels it is a burden and a problem and not a life-giving reality? He fails to recognize that his faith is a «Yes» converting impulse.

But, in fact, faith is a «Yes» of that kind even when the believer cannot rationally explain his choice or forsee where it will lead. In faith he sacrifices his selfish independence and transcends his rationalism. Of course, the paradox is that nothing is lost, but all is gained.

The first move is always God's, God searches for man. The essence of Christianity, insofar as it is first and foremost a religion, consists in man's recognition of his dependence on God. Strictly speaking, it is not faith that justifies, but God who justifies by means of faith. Faith extends itself through hope and charity. So I suppose we should say that this indifference we are speaking about, this freedom, is a yearning inside a man to say «Yes» to God as God moves him interiorly. It is a desire to sell all that one has to buy the field, or to get the pearl of great price.

Knowledge that one is loved by God is a prerequisite for this freedom. I do not see how a man could ask for this freedom unless he had an awareness that God loved him. Now, there is a kind of parallel in a child with his father or mother. The child has a kind of freedom in faith towards what the father or mother asks of him. But again that is in a love context, is it not? For youngsters, their parents' love is an expression of God's love.

I just suggested that you cannot even present this truth to a person unless he has experienced God's love. We considered earlier whether a person could appreciate God's love for him if he had not experienced some kind of human love. I would not want to say outright that he could not because I do not think you can control the Holy Spirit. But the Spirit ordinarily operates in a human context. Therefore, unless the person had received some kind of human love, he is not going to be able to appreciate God's love.

It has been my experience with some individuals whose experience of human love was rather limited that they were quite capable of comparing that meagre love with the love of the crucified Lord. In meditating on the crucified Lord, they were overwhelmed by his expression of love for them. In that context, then, they were ready to move, and they gained their freedom.

I remember the change in one person especially. I was not the only one to see the change. A group of men who had known him for years were on retreat with this man, and they could not get over the way he had changed. Even his facial expression and his whole attitude was transformed. All of a sudden he had become free. The basic experience was the deep realization that God loved him. It had been gained mostly through prayer to our Lord hanging on the cross. He was deeply moved by Paul's words: «what proves that God loves us is that Christ died for us while we were still sinners.» (Rm 5:8) His experience of human love had not had the power to free him as did that simple prayer before the crucified Lord.

Another prerequisite for this kind of freedom is prayer to the

Holy Spirit. You are seeking what is solely a gift from God. The Lord said: «the Holy Spirit, whom the Father will send in my name, will teach you everything and remind you of all I have said to you.» (Jn 14:26) Another saying of the Lord is that, «The truth shall set you free.» And what is the basic truth that makes us free? It is that God loves us with an overwhelming love. It follows that my prayer on this part of the «Principle and Foundation» is to ask the interior Spirit to make me aware of this love, to help me to «abide in God's love,» and thus give me that trust to surrender in all freedom to the will of God for me, knowing that this will is in conformity to my true self.

CHAPTER 4

DIRECTING ANOTHER'S PRAYER

May the God of our Lord Jesus Christ, the Father of glory, give you a spirit of wisdom and perception of what is revealed, to bring you to full knowledge of him. May he enlighten the eyes of your mind so that you can see what hope his call holds for you, what rich glories he has promised the saints will inherit and how infinitely great is the power that he has exercised for us believers. This you can tell from the strength of his power at work in Christ, when he used it to raise him from the dead and to make him sit at his right hand, in heaven, far above every Sovereignty, Authority, Power, or Domination, or any other name that can be named, not only in this age but also in the age to come. (Eph 1:17-21)

Counseling a person in the spiritual life requires a context of prayer. In fact, it is very difficult to give spiritual direction to someone who is not seriously trying to pray. Moreover, it is helpful to know the subject of his prayer. One of the advantages of a retreat is that, because you know what material the retreatant is considering, you can give him counsel in full awareness of the context of his prayer. It follows, I think, that outside the time of retreat a director ought to inquire about his client's spiritual reading, habitual methods of prayer, and about any movements and changes that may be occurring in his personal relations with God.

Most people know by experience how difficult it can be to open oneself up to another. It is hard enough to talk about one's psychological condition. Even going to a doctor can be an occasion for embarrassment or reluctance. Well, it is more difficult to initiate discussion of one's spiritual life.

The easiest way, or the gentlest way, is for the counselor to begin by asking the counselee what he is praying about and how the prayer is going. It can be useful in direction if the counselee makes known what Scripture passages, or texts from the Exercises, or whatever he is praying over. But in any case it is only in the context of his prayer that good spiritual direction can be given. Inevitably, counseling will soon come around to the topic of prayer.

The counselor should begin, therefore, by asking what his client is praying about and will probably end by giving him new material to use. Ignatius provides a few specific directions in the early pages of the *Spiritual Exercises* that are important for any prayer context. He calls them «Annotations.» I would like to comment on some that I think are more important.

Ignatius asks the director to give a very limited amount of material to the person who is praying:

> The reason for this is that when one in meditating takes the solid foundation of facts, and goes over it and reflects on it for himself, he may find something that makes them a little clearer or better understood. This may arise either from his own reasoning, or from the grace of God enlightening his mind. Now this produces greater spiritual relish and fruit than if one in giving the Exercises had explained and developed the meaning at great length. For it is not much knowledge that fills and satisfies the soul, but the intimate understanding and relish of the truth. [2]

In other words, what is important is not to get through a great deal of subject matter in prayer but to grasp profoundly whatever one prays about. *Non multa sed multum.*

Good retreat directors do not give very much material for prayer. Most of them I suspect, ask the retreatant to pray over a few verses of Scripture or an exercise. Thus, it is much better if the retreatant can tell the director what individual, personal motions and reactions have occurred in prayer rather than simply to repeat to the director what had previously been given to him.

Another instruction of Ignatius reads: «It will be very profitable for the one who is to go through the Exercises to enter upon them with magnanimity and generosity toward his Creator and Lord, and to offer Him his entire will and liberty, that His Divine Majesty may dispose of him and all he possesses according to His most holy will.» [5] Even one's first entry into prayer requires a tremendous offering of oneself. Here already there is the recognition of an interpersonal relationship with the indwelling Spirit. Ignatius's directives indicate that the exercitant may experience this relationship in consolation or desolation. When there is no experience of consolation or desolation, the director is to inquire carefully into the reasons for this lack of experience. [*cf.* 6, 7]

Again, «if the director of the Exercises observes that the exercitant is in desolation and tempted, let him not deal severely and harshly with him, but gently and kindly.» [7] There are times, of course, when a director is obliged to be very forceful with his client, as Ignatius suggests elsewhere. [*cf.* 6] Even then his true kindness and gentleness should be in evidence. But when a retreatant is struggling with serious difficulties, Ignatius wants the director to be especially sympathetic and encouraging: «He should encourage and strengthen him for the future by exposing to him the wiles of the enemy of our human nature, and by getting him to prepare and dispose himself for the coming consolation.» [7] These are good directives for anyone counseling another within a context of prayer, whether on retreat or outside the time of retreat.

It is not helpful for a counselor to see his client too often. We should note Ignatius's advice on this. [2] Even during the Exercises it is questionable whether the director should see his retreatant twice a day.

The one who is praying is the Lord's friend more than yours. Many of the difficulties you think you are handling, the Holy Spirit can handle much better. As much as you do not want the person to suffer and to anguish, there is a place for suffering and anguish in religious life as the individual surrenders himself to the demands of Christ. You have to be careful not to become a crutch for the one who comes to you for direction.

In fact, you can be cruel to the person by not leaving him alone. The director is not Jesus Christ. He has to let the Lord operate. His role is to point out the Lord and then get out of the way. St. John the Baptist points the way for spiritual directors in his words concerning Christ: «He must grow greater. I must grow smaller.» (Jn 3:30)

Annotation 14 considers a danger that may threaten a generous person when he makes the Exercises. In a moment of enthusiasm he may make some rash promise or vow. A wise director will delay him in this and ask questions about the origin or causes of his desire. It is not the place of the director to suggest things to him one way or another, but rather to let the Creator inspire this person. «But while one is engaged in the Spiritual Exercises, it is more suitable and much better that the Creator and Lord in person communicate Himself to the devout soul in quest of the divine will, that He inflame it with His love

59

and praise, and dispose it for the way in which it could better serve God in the future.» [15]

To stand off and be patient and objective, as experience shows, is a very difficult role to maintain. This is because the interpersonal relationship in spiritual counseling can become very close indeed. There is always a tendency for the director to want his client to obtain the grace he needs as soon as possible. But perhaps a growth of many days (or, outside retreat, of many months or years) will be required.

In situations like these there is a real danger of interfering with the Holy Spirit. As he strives to assist the work of the Spirit, the director, too, needs to be indifferent: «Therefore, the director of the Exercises, as a balance at equilibrium, without leaning to one side or the other, should permit the Creator to deal directly with the creature, and the creature directly with his Creator and Lord.» [15]

Ignatius cautions the director that he does not need to know the details of a person's sinful life:

> While the one who is giving the Exercises should not seek to investigate and know the private thoughts and sins of the exercitant, nevertheless, it will be very helpful if he is kept faithfully informed about the various disturbances and thoughts caused by the action of different spirits. This will enable him to propose some spiritual exercises in accordance with the degree of progress made and suited and adapted to the needs of a soul disturbed in this way.» [17]

The retreatant's sinful past is not really the point in the Exercises. [cf. 15]

Instead, the director should be interested in how the person has been moved in the prayer experience. Has he felt an uplift of soul or is he depressed? Has he experienced the grace being sought or not? For the purposes of the Exercises, the answers to these questions are much more important than his past sinful life.

Equally important are the temptations and other sorts of disturbances that may arise. These movements within the retreatant are part of the mystery that is the Exercises. Many of them may be quite new and unexpected to the exercitant himself, but the director should never be caught by surprise — such experiences are common enough. Right in the middle of a thirty-day retreat, a person may have some of the most vivid sexual disturbances and temptations of his life. But they are only temptations. They are not sinful and he should not get upset over them. However, the director needs to know about them in order to discern what spirit is moving the retreatant.

Outside the time of retreat, prayer is usually experienced much less intensely. All the same, various sorts of disturbances may trouble a counselee from time to time or recurrently in his prayer or in his reading and his efforts to find God in all things. I think that the ascetical principles set forth by Ignatius here can be adapted easily enough to those situations.

Normally Ignatius does not want the exercitant to receive the sacrament of penance from the one who is directing him. Nevertheless, in some instances the sacrament of penance can become an instrument for openness, and through it the director may get to know the person a little better. Some people feel more at ease in a confession situation.

But confessing one's sins is not really the point of the Exercises. They are not an examination into one's sinful life in order to prepare for the sacrament of penance. They have a different purpose, as we have seen, namely to bring the exercitant to a condition of freedom. A knowledge of interior movements in the retreatant, whether temptations to sin or calls to virtue, helps to gain the purpose of the Exercises.

Obviously, a similar acquaintance with the inner life of the counselee is important in any sort of counseling. But a distinction can be made between material for confession and material for spiritual direction. When a man commits a sin, whatever it is, he has consented to it and has done it; it is his own act. But in prayer or under spiritual direction there are interior movements which he does not and cannot produce himself. The director is interested, not in a confession of the person's free acts which incur guilt, but rather in what is happening to the person.

This distinction should be useful for sisters. Since they are not ordained they do not have the sacramental powers of absolution. They may have, however, the ability to discern what is happening to a person in prayer and to help the person understand himself more deeply. The director should be concerned about the basic disorder in one's life, the good and bad tendencies that can be seen. He wants the person to recognize these tendencies and to understand himself or herself and in that sense become an instrument for the Lord. In the long run, these tendencies may be much more important than sins.

A problem arises if you are not a priest and in the course of a retreat an exercitant wishes to discuss a matter of conscience. In such a case, I would say it depends a great deal on who is talking to whom. If you feel that your client is quite relaxed in relating his sinfulness to you, let him do so. You should be very careful to discover whether or not this has anything to do with his prayer life. If it has nothing to do with it, you say: «Well, look, that's not really important in this context of prayer. Let's get down to what's important. What happened in your prayer?»

In a retreat, the important thing is what is happening here and now. It is true that a man brings his sinful past with him into retreat. But the past matters only insofar as its effects perdure into the present in some way. You have to make that very clear to the person you are directing. It may be necessary for him to open up some part of his life to you. But I think you should say initially, «I don't really want to know that part. That is the work of a confessor.» Sometimes it is difficult to distinguish confessional matter from directional matter. The important thing is whether and how the person is being moved. Then the director can see if the person is opening up at the same time that he is confessing.

Since the question of confession has entered this discussion, perhaps it will be in order at this point to make some brief comments on that sacrament and on external penances. In the *Exercises*, Ignatius deals with both subjects in conjunction with the first week. [44, 82, 87]

Because the sacraments are an extension of the Incarnation, our spiritual lives need to be renewed repeatedly, not only through nourishment in the Eucharist, but through reconciliation with God as well. My own experience is that once in a while, whether I have committed a serious sin or not, I feel the need for the sacrament of penance. I suppose it is the Spirit drawing me back to the Father. In any case, I do need to experience the actual forgiveness of Christ.

One way to understand this sacrament of forgiveness is to consider how one person approaches another. We approach each other in many different ways and on many different levels. For example, at times we go to a friend in order to share a confidence, to learn his reaction to new events, or to find sympathy and understanding — to be strengthened and consoled by him. At other times we might go to him very humbly because we realize we need his forgiveness.

I think it is the same with Christ. A man can approach him in the Eucharist as a friend. At other times he might come to him as the only one who can forgive his sins. And in this search for forgiveness, only a personal contact with Christ can satisfy the need that is felt. It is not enough to seek forgiveness interiorly or at the Eucharist. More than that, one wants to hear the human representative of Christ say, «I absolve you from your sins.» This sacrament, like all sacraments, is an interpersonal affair. Grace does not come to us like water poured into an empty vessel — coldly and impersonally. The closer we are to the Lord, the more we may feel the need for this sacrament.

We always approach Jesus Christ as a friend, but he is a special kind of friend because he can forgive sins. Another friend can forgive the offense that one has committed against him, but he cannot forgive the sin that lurks beneath it. A human friend cannot heal what I have done to myself, but Christ can do just that. He can give to one who is sorry for selfish sins a new power of selflessness.

Some priests can help some people to meet Christ, the forgiving friend, more easily than others can. If a man finds such a priest, I suppose this would determine how often he goes to confession. Yet there are situations when the soul is crying out for absolution. Then any priest becomes a God-send. This is when there is a real, existential need for absolution.

Penances, too, are best understood in the personal relationship with Christ. Ignatius gives three principal reasons for external penance: to make satisfaction for past sins, to overcome oneself, and to obtain some grace or gift that one earnestly desires. [87]

We might consider the first as belonging to the unitive way, a means of uniting oneself with the suffering Christ, an act of love. How does satisfaction for sin come about? Through the sufferings of Christ as a part of the repairing act of the paschal mystery. In Paul's mind the redemptive act continues through the mystical body: «I am suffering now, and in my own body... do what I can to make up all that has still to be undergone by Christ for the sake of his body, the Church.» (Col 1:24) Thus, I can see my union with Christ in his sufferings through penance as an aspect of the unitive way.

In the second reason for doing penance, I think Ignatius is referring to the *agere contra* principle (this will be discussed more in chapter 11). As is often true with the *agere contra,* some people tend to make penance an end in itself. But the interpersonal context ought to have some bearing here as well.

Often during spiritual direction the client will mention, as the cause of a sinful or imperfect act, a certain lack of control. And he will ask: «How do I handle this?» In your discussion of different ways you might suggest a little penance.

The third reason for penance is petition. Here, again, we might remember the whole person is involved in prayer. Penance, in this instance, would suggest a more earnest desire involving the body as well as the soul in seeking some grace from the Lord.

In setting up a continuing prayer experience for someone on retreat, the overall pattern is more important than the particular Scripture from which the retreatant may select his own prayer material. But for crucial moments in the evolving pattern you should give him the core texts that you think will best present the movement of spirits normally expected in any retreat.

The basic pattern for a retreat will begin with the question, «Who am I?» (This would incorporate material from the «Principle and Foundation.») At once there follows the time of *puri-*

fication from sin in the context of God's forgiving love, which motivates the exercitant to outgoing, responsible, mature love (First Week). The time of *orientation* will involve some new understanding of self and the discernment of spirits in our world (Second Week). Finally, *confirmation* is given in the presence of Christ through suffering and joy, and this includes hope of integration and meaning in one's life (Third and Fourth Week). You will naturally be careful in choosing the texts you think best for these core experiences, but alternative texts will be useful to insure that the retreatant has freedom even in this matter.

Thus, in keeping with this basic pattern, an eight-day retreat might be planned as follows: The first day is a day of rest and quiet with some praying and thinking about the «Principle and Foundation.» Then a couple of days should be devoted to sin. Next, a consideration of the call to be with Christ and to labor with him. There might follow one-and-a-half days on Christ's public life: this will mean praying over the demands, the self-commitment urged upon those who love the Lord — requirements crystallized in the «Two Standards,» the «Three Classes of Men» and the «Three Degrees of Humility.» Finally, three days with Christ, dying and rising, and the «Contemplation to Attain Love of God.»

More and more, it is the experience of many here at Guelph that seldom can you introduce the key meditations of the Exercises — «Kingdom,» «Two Standards,» «Three Classes of Men,» «Three Degrees of Humility» — to a person who is making his first eight-day directed retreat. With such a person a better pattern would present the retreatant with the matter of the «Principle and Foundation» and the «First Week.» The material of the last day might be Christ's triumph over sin and death — the Paschal Mystery.

Ignatius's instructions on prayer, both for the director and the exercitant, are basically intended to enable a person to adopt a reverent but trusting and open attitude before his Creator and Lord. Thus, the director is to give brief rather than long points and not to inquire in detail into the person's sinful life. The approach to the sacrament of penance, both from the director's and the exercitant's standpoint should promote freedom for the Spirit to operate.

Similarly, the carefully detailed additions that Ignatius gives for recollection, [78-81] preparation for prayer, [73-75] and position in prayer [76] are also to aid the generous person to free himself and be reverent before the Lord. His explanation and instructions on the use of interior and exterior penance are in keeping with the purpose of the Exercises, which is «the conquest of self and the regulation of one's life in such a way that no decision is made under the influence of any inordinate attachment.» [21] These brief annotations and additions should be kept in mind no matter how short or long the prayer program may be and no matter what particular aim is intended.

Ignatius wants the retreatant to make a fifteen-minute review of his success or failure in the previous exercise. He is to seek out the causes for each. If his prayer was a success, he is to give thanks and try to follow the same method next time. [77]

The review of prayer is basic for a continuing prayer program. Ignatius indicates this in explaining the repetitions of previous exercises. [62, 118] Thus, in reviewing his last prayer period, the person can determine where he has met the Lord most forcefully, either in consolation or desolation. This, then, will help him decide on the prayer material for his next period.

It is important to remember that the review takes place after the prayer period, not during it. In the midst of the prayer itself one should not be constantly examining how things are going. A distraction of that sort would leave no place for the

Spirit. One needs to enter into prayer with a simple heart and let the hour proceed in direct contact with the Lord. During the time of prayer one has to be relaxed enough to let the Spirit operate. The discerning process usually occurs after the prayer experience. He can then look back and ask, «How am I being moved and by whom? Is it the Holy Spirit?» He should be concerned about what is consciously happening. One has to enter prayer with a certain freedom and then let it go.

CHAPTER 5.

SIN AND SALVATION

We were still helpless when at his appointed moment
Christ died for sinful men. It is not easy to die, even for
a good man — though of course for someone really
worthy, a man might be prepared to die — but what
proves that God loves us is that Christ died for us while
we were still sinners. Having died to make us righteous,
is it likely that he would now fail to save us from God's
anger? When we were reconciled to God by the death
of his Son, we were still enemies; now that we have been
reconciled, surely we may count on being saved by the
life of his Son? Not merely because we have been
reconciled but because we are filled with joyful trust in
God, through our Lord Jesus Christ, through whom we
have already gained our reconciliation. (Rm 5:6-11)

In spiritual counseling one of the most basic considerations is sin. How does your client see sin? How does he
experience the mercy of God? These are important questions
when you are giving spiritual direction.

People are «hung up» on sin in a different way than you
would expect. They think it means they are not lovable. But
what it really means is that they are not loving. These are different things. We are always lovable, because God loves us. In fact,
one of the main aims of the exercises on sin is to come to a
realization of the unfailing love of God. Another is to keep

us from offending a God who is so good.

By now we realize that most of the meditations and prayers in the Exercises are intended to move us out of ourselves. Even though there is a tremendous amount of introspection in the prayers on sin, they are still directed towards the all-loving, all-merciful God. I think this must be stressed because our whole background has convinced us that being loved depends on producing results. We imagine that we must do something good before people will love us, before even God will love us. This pelagian tendency is very strong.

The mystery about human beings is that they are lovable, whether or not they are doing good things. The meditations on sin are intended to impart a deep awareness of the fact that, sinful as a man is, he is loved.

Nevertheless, the exercises of the «First Week» are very difficult, dwelling as they do on all that is evil in man and in man's world. Thinking exclusively about his sins would tend to fill a man with loathing for himself. It could become very depressing. But the whole purpose of these exercises is to free him from his sinful self and to center his heart and mind on the good merciful God, his Father.

Ignatius calls this «First Exercise» of the «First Week» a «meditation,» and, as is true whenever he introduces a new method of prayer, he explains it in detail. Meditation is the application of the memory, intellect, and will to revealed truths.

As a preliminary to the prayer, he gives a «composition of place»; perhaps it might be better termed a «composition of the person.» As he describes it, the composition seems strange indeed: «to see in imagination my soul as a prisoner in this corruptible body, and to consider my whole composite being as an exile here on earth, cast out to live among brute beasts. I said my whole composite being, body and soul.» [47]

Well, that is a pretty terrible picture. And «corruptible body»: I suppose for most of us that stirs up an image of ulcers and all sorts of decay, something like the picture of Dorian Gray. But, all Ignatius means, I think, is that it is a body destined to decay and die. In that sense it is «corruptible.»

The point to be aimed at here, I believe, is a deeper sense of the impotency, the helplessness of man. And so he is to place himself in a position of being helpless and enslaved, as though he were chained to a chair, for example. He becomes directly conscious of his separation from God.

But, even more than separation from God, there is borne in on him his inability to free himself from this enslavement. It resembles the image of the prodigal son in the foreign land. He has been enslaved by his sensual desires; he is an alien in a foreign land; he cannot make himself understood. Moreover, because he is surrounded by animals, he is isolated from human sympathy. He is cut off from his friends. The first movement toward his father comes when he experiences hunger. Only then does he realize he is a sinner.

The frightening thing about all this is that man is the cause of his own enslavement; he enslaves himself. And that stirs up more bitterness, and more discouragement and more frustration, as he discovers the particular ways in which his own sins are enslaving him. This reaction can come from the devil in the sense that it leads to more and more pride, more and more concern for oneself, more and more setting oneself up against the whole world, the universe, and even against God.

Ignatius directs the retreatant to seek a special grace in each exercise. Eventually the retreatant becomes conscious that the petition for grace and the colloquy are the two most important parts of each exercise. He may feel that what he seeks is totally beyond him; yet the Lord asks him to pray, and the Lord is never outdone in generosity.

In the second prelude, «I will ask God our Lord for what I want and desire. ... Here it will be to ask for shame and confusion, because I see how many have been lost on account of a single mortal sin, and how many times I have deserved eternal damnation, because of the many grievous sins that I have committed.» [48] He asks for shame and confusion, although this is a meditation on three sins that are not his doing.

The angels sinned; Adam and Eve sinned; another person sinned. These sins are external to the retreatant. As transitory actions they no longer exist; in fact, in some theologies of great repute, sin has no positive reality. It is absurd in the radical sense: it has no intelligence. Hence it can never be present to man as is the risen Christ in the mysterious entity which is his Body.

The retreatant cannot contemplate these sins as he contemplates Christ in his present reality. But he can ponder God's judgment on these sinners and contrast it with the treatment he has received in view of what he knows he deserves. In this way Ignatius involves him with Adam and Eve and the rebel angels and this sinful *alter ego*. From this involvement, by God's grace, there should arise in his heart shame and confusion in the face of goodness and generosity.

What Ignatius means by «shame and confusion» is best seen from the parallel with a son who has offended his loving father. The son is aware of his father's goodness and love; he knows too that he has offended his father. And still his father responds with love. The son feels embarrassed in the face of such goodness.

This is quite different from the experience of being caught in a mistake. It is not merely that the culprit is exposed. Rather, his negative response to goodness signifies a failure at the deepest level of his personhood. He cannot cope with it; it is beyond him. He is ashamed and confused.

In the «First Exercise» shame and confusion manifest themselves by means of a series of comparisons. The retreatant compares himself with Satan and his sin. He compares himself with Adam and Eve. He compares himself with someone else who has committed one sin. He compares his situation with that of these sinners. He has Christ, he has his death on the cross, he has his sacraments; the angels did not, nor did Adam and Eve. He seeks, then, to know deep shame in the face of his Father's unfailing goodness, to see the stark contrast between what he has deserved and how he has been loved.

Embarrassment, shame, and confusion are non-intellectual things. They can be described to another, but, when he experiences them, they are not the same as an intellectual insight. They are something a man feels. I usually express this to other people by saying that in my own being I experience that God loves me more than any other person who has ever existed. That is what I want to experience when meditating on sin. It is my subjective awareness of God's love for me.

A dramatic way of expressing this awareness might be to say that I feel God loves me more than he loves anyone else, even the Blessed Virgin Mary. What do I mean by that? Obviously, our Lady's participation in God's love has given her an exalted position. But in my experience, which is uniquely my own, I am more highly loved than she. Of course, in her individual way, she has no competitors either.

And every other person has his own unique experience of God and God's love for him. A homely example might show this. If you ask a mother whether she loves one child more than another, she will say, «No, but I love them all differently, each in his own way.» The experience of each child is unique. (I am presuming here a healthy home life where love dominates the family.) Each child, on reflection, can feel confident that the mother loves him or her — in that unique manner — more than the others.

The graces we seek make us realize that each of us is, in a special way, a favorite of God. We know God does not have favorites; God loves everyone to the extent of his being. But my experience is that I am the favorite one; I am the graced one. In a sense I feel I am more graced even than our Lady.

I think this explains the comparison in the sin meditation. Everyone knows he has not cooperated with grace in the past. In many instances grace has prevented him from committing terrible sins. When a man contrasts the way God seems to have treated everyone else with the way God has treated him, he is overwhelmed with shame and confusion that God has treated him better than he has the others.

For a person to say, «God loves me more than anyone else,» sounds like a very proud statement. In fact, the case is just the opposite. He is experiencing grace. The experience of grace is the experience of being loved. When a man is loved by God or when he is loved by another human being, he does not have any control over it. It is very humbling! He says, «My God, Why?» He cannot believe it is happening because he has not cooperated or done anything; he is just there. But he knows he is loved, and he knows he could not produce it, much less deserve it. He does not control the situation. It just happens. And it seems to me that, far from making one proud, it humbles a person to the very ground.

Humility is always the response to the mystery of being loved. It helps to explain why the greatest lovers, the saints, thought they were the greatest sinners, that is, non-lovers. I think they were so overwhelmed with the intensity of love received that what others might consider a slight offense, they felt was a great refusal of grace. It is to this point of view that Ignatius leads us in the Exercises.

When a man receives the grace of shame and confusion as he compares how he has been loved with what he deserves, then he can shout with St. Paul, «For I am certain of this: neither death nor life, no angel, no prince, nothing that exists, nothing still to come, not any power, or height or depth, nor any created thing, can ever come between us and the love of God made visible in Christ Jesus our Lord.» (Rm 8:38, 39) But sometimes he fails to gain the shame and confusion that he desires. This does not mean God is not loving him. God always loves him. Perhaps he is not experiencing the love of God at the moment and his temporary coldness prevents him from getting this sense of shame and confusion. He cannot produce in himself an overwhelming awareness of how much God loves him.

When this occurs, we can see more clearly what is meant by grace. Grace is a free gift in the same way that love is a free gift. Just as you cannot compel another person to love you, so also you cannot force grace from God. When a man and woman love each other, their love comes as an unexpected gift; when a member of my community loves me, I know that I receive what I could not demand. But always in love it is not some object or token that a person gives; it is himself.

In the same way, grace is not an object or a token; it is the personal communication of God himself to us. It is the Spirit's presence in us. And yet our liberty is delicately maintained. God does not come suddenly before a person to confront him with his powerful love. Love is free both in the giving and receiving. In fact, the reception of love actually makes a man free. Man finds himself within the love of God, within the sphere of the Trinity's love. To freely accept a gift so freely given enables him to love in the way that divine Persons love — in perfect freedom.

It is in terms of a love like this that man can ask for shame and confusion at not responding. The very prayer itself, even the desire to pray is already the action of the Spirit. As Paul says in Romans, «The Spirit too comes to help us in our weakness. For when we cannot choose words in order to pray properly, the Spirit himself expresses our plea in a way that could never be put into words.» (Rm 8:26)

The reason why I have spoken of a person's feeling «more graced» than anyone else can be seen in the comparison proposed by Ignatius in the «First Exercise»: «I see how many have been lost on account of a single mortal sin and how many times I have deserved eternal damnation, because of the many grievous sins that I have committed.»[48]

Because each one has a unique relationship with God and because God is infinite in his love, there is a sense in which no comparison is possible. But the point really is that man is overwhelmed by the love that God showers upon him. For the most part, he cannot see into the hearts of others. But he deeply experiences God's love for himself. When, therefore, he considers the external treatment meted out to other men, God's love for him seems greater than his love for anyone else. He does not deserve to be loved like this. After this awareness has come over him, perhaps he will no longer want to make comparisons but will prefer simply to let himself be overwhelmed by the infinity of love that God has given him.

He has to acknowledge the presence of sin and disorder in himself, and yet he sees that somehow their devastating effects have been withheld. When he looks at the miserable effects of sin and disorder in other people and in the universe, the comparison strikes home. Then he begins to appreciate that God loves him in a way that he has never known before.

Even on the natural level, why is it some people are crippled or retarded? Why are whole areas hit by tidal waves or swept by epidemics? Why do thousands of people lose everything at once, and why are thousands suddenly crushed to death — in all the abject misery that we witness uncomfortably on our television screens? Why should it not happen to me, disordered creature that I know myself to be? From my human experience, from the experience I have of this world, I can make that comparison. It underscores my feeling that God has shown more patience and compassion and love to me than he has to others.

Moreover, no individual knows for sure if others have sinned. He knows that he himself has sinned, and he is uniquely aware that God has showered him with the special love that is necessary to take away the destructive force of his sin. Within the context of God's real love for him, which he experiences now, he can with confidence pray for the grace to realize that what he in fact deserves is to be separated forever from God. Ignatius does not want any trace of smugness to remain.

God is eager to forgive us and to give himself to us. Does the sinner really know that? In his prayer he seeks to appreciate the mystery of sin, of his own helplessness, and of the forgiving love of God. In our ordinary lives we take this all too much for granted. Even the fact that we can petition in prayer for knowledge of our sins is given to us unbidden. To know that we are sinners, and that love comes to us even in our sinfulness, is a tremendous mystery.

Thus, Ignatius sets up the «First Exercise» as a meditation on three sins: the sin of the angels, the sin of Adam and Eve, the sin of another person. This meditation does not involve the retreatant directly in his personal sins; that consideration is delayed until the following exercise. The «First Exercise» is a study of sin itself, what it is and what it does. A searchlight is focused on the terrible disorder that flows from sin.

Now, it is true that, when a man considers this meditation carefully, he sees the larger context of sin. It is not a study of sin alone, but it includes the fact that God has treated him differently than he has treated anyone else on the face of the earth.

One of my friends once mentioned that our Lady could make the «First Exercise.» I am not sure about the «Second Exercise,» but she could make the first one, because she would realize the special love that God bestows upon her. That love prevented her from committing sin in the first place, and preserves her in favor always. And so she would be overwhelmed with gratitude, which is the end-product of this exercise.

These three sins the exercitant relives in himself. Usually he is guilty of the sin of pride as truly as are the angels. They wanted to determine their own life, and they wanted to be worshipped rather than to love. They wanted to be lovable rather than to love. These are the very reversals of reality brought about by sin in ordinary people.

And each of us, like Adam and Eve, wishes to determine for himself what is good and what is evil. That is another form of pride. We, too, wish to set up our own code of morals. We want our selfish use of sex, our greed for possessions, our efforts to dominate or manipulate others into exclusive rights of our own. In the sin of Adam and Eve we see the usual dynamism of sin.

We see its influence grow in Cain to the point that he kills his brother Abel. «Am I my brother's keeper?» Cain wants to determine for himself what is good and evil. And this dynamic keeps on spreading and increasing until we come to the Biblical account of Noah. By then it is very difficult to find a just man.

For all these reasons Ignatius asks the person to meditate on the sin of the angels and the sin of Adam and Eve. Today there are various interpretations of the Biblical account: some ask whether or not angels exist, whether or not Adam and Eve existed. If questions of this sort distract the exercitant's mind, then we must find some other instrument to get the comparison across. The sin of David (2 S 11:1 — 12:15) might be a good consideration.

The important thing, I think, is to understand what this meditation is trying to accomplish and to supply prayer material that will be effective. As usual, many people today — including people devoted to their faith — do not deeply realize their sinfulness. They receive strong encouragement in this from the unbelief that surrounds their lives. Many philosophers and psychologists do not believe there is such a thing as sin. For some, the sense of sin is lost when God becomes only a vague idea. For others, God means a sense of duty, or doing good, or living the good life. It is easy enough to reduce God to an impersonal «deity.»

For those under the heady influence of Rousseau, evil comes from oppressive social structures alone. Left to himself, man is impeccable, sinless. For this «noble savage» (despite all the evidence since Rousseau's day), no effort at self-control or self-possession is needed. Simply let every individual do his own thing. Put him in the countryside and he will be good and loving. Why should he look for forgiveness or mercy?

Moreover, for many people there is no such thing as an erroneous conscience; there is only a justifying conscience. Morality is reduced to the pragmatic: actions are correct if they work. This easily slips into «not being caught.» But, in any case, a man's relationship with the personal God is out of the question.

Then there are those who say that man is sinful but not a sinner. Sin is reduced to compulsion, to temperament, to sexual drive, to the environment, or to upbringing. Since he is totally a victim of circumstances, he is free of any guilt.

Claudel said that the greatest sin is to lose the sense of sin. The knowledge that sin exists and that man is a sinner can come only from revelation; it is a grace. Forgiveness, too, is a grace. In the act of forgiving God is revealing himself to man as merciful, and he reveals man to himself as justified. In every act of forgiveness he meets the God whom Moses met and knew as «Yahweh, a God of tenderness and compassion, slow to anger, rich in kindness and faithfulness.» (Ex 34:6)

This meditation on the triple sin is set in a cosmic context: the sphere of the angels, the world-shaking origins of man — of Everyman. This cosmic dimension returns in the «Call of the King,» in the «Two Standards,» and in the mystery of the resurrection. Because sin is the foe of God, and the enemy of human nature its wider setting must be known. To join him in the struggle against sin is the challenge given to man by Christ the King. Man is called to combat, not only the sin in his own life, but the sin and disorder in the universe as well.

One result of original sin is spiritual impotence for what is good. As Paul says in Romans, «instead of doing the good things I want to do, I carry out the sinful things I do not want.» (Rm 7:19) Original sin seems to build into our moral nature a certain unwillingness, and inability to respond spontaneously to our own good. There is a kind of inertia which comes with original sin. This is the disorder that you experience as a member of the human race.

The sin of the angels is a very important sin to pray over because it clarifies the inner nature of sin. In past generations sin was almost always equated with the sex act or with the sins of the flesh. The sin of the angels emphasizes that sin is of the spirit, not of the body — and that is a good and necessary corrective.

The third sin needs more consideration: «In like manner, we are to do the same with regard to the third sin, namely, that of one who went to hell because of one mortal sin. Consider also countless others who have been lost for fewer sins than I have committed. I said to do the same for the third particular sin. Recall to memory the gravity and malice of sin against our Creator and Lord.» [52]

We do not know for sure if there is anyone in hell. In any case, I think the best way to handle this third point is to focus on oneself. It is possible to stand outside oneself and look at oneself objectively. «Should I not be there in hell? I should be there. Why am I not in hell? What have I deserved? Why has sin not been allowed to follow its course in me?» Sin is basically destructive. Sin starts with an act of rejection of God's love. It starts with an act of hatred of God. «Why is it that the dynamism of sin has not been allowed to find completion in me?» For hell is sin's ultimate success. «What prevented me from sliding into hell?» In our prayer we can certainly do this. We can stand outside ourselves and look at our life, be objective with respect to ourselves, and stand in amazement.

Because love is a great mystery the rejection of love is a great mystery too. Somehow, in fact, it seems to be a greater mystery. How can one reject love? But we know some men actually do. Despite these stupefying rejections, God returns to his weak, sinful creatures, and he showers even more love on them. How difficult it is to grasp this! That is why in these meditations one comes to some appreciation of the extreme love of God. As St. Paul said in the passage already cited, «While we were his enemies, he loved us.»

This becomes the great sign of a Christian who has experienced forgiveness — he can love his enemies. It is also, of course, a great sign of grace, a gift of the Lord, to be able to love one's enemy. In Luke the Lord says, «love your enemies and do good, ... and you will be sons of the Most High, for he himself is kind to the ungrateful and the wicked.» (Lk 6:35) It is a tremendous sign of grace.

And that is what this exercise is all about, to recognize oneself as a forgiven enemy of God. A good scriptural passage for this exercise is in Peter's second letter. (2P 2:1-22) The passage deserves to be studied for it sums up this whole meditation. In addition, there are a number of references to Satan in John, who presents our Lord in confrontation with the forces of evil, (*cf.* Jn 6:70; 8:44; 12:31; 13:2,27) an evil that is greater than that of the scribes and pharisees. It is well to remember, when difficulties arise with this exercise, that «The devil... is a liar, and the Father of lies.» (Jn 8:45)

Now the «First Exercise» takes up the question of the punishment for sin. This confuses many people who think the punishment for sin is imposed by God. In one sense it is, since he keeps us in being and allows the punishment to happen. But punishment is intrinsic to sin; it is sin that destroys the sinner. This is why people do not like to meditate on sin: they do not want to be confronted with their own responsibility for sin and its effects. Sin is destructive; it brings disorder. It brings with it hate and selfishness and all comparable evils.

Moreover, sin reduces the sinner to impotence. When man has committed sin, he is helpless by his own deed. Now it is very important for him to know all this; otherwise, he will not understand the kindness and mercy of God. Only by experiencing these truths deeply in prayer will he come to appreciate God's saving act.

Our image of God can influence our whole approach to sin. Since we are usually unwilling to look at the negative side of our existence, we rarely see the helplessness and impotency of

82

our condition before God forgives us. But this is often combined with a distorted image of God. He is portrayed in wrath and anger driving men and women into the smoky abyss of hell. In this version of hell, God is supposed to be vigorously pursuing man for his sins.

In another twisted doctrine some Christians speak of Christ as saving men by hanging on the cross before God the Father. When God looks down on sinful mankind, all he sees is Christ hanging there. He cannot see sinful men because they are hidden behind the crucified Christ. In this way Christ manages to save men from hell. What a terrible picture of God the Father!

But what is the truth? It is that Christ interposes himself between sinful mankind and hell. As a sinner man is impotent, so he cannot save himself. But Christ can! Jesus Christ, therefore, is hanging not between man and the Father, but between man and hell. The Father's love reaches out to man. It is the Father who sent his Son to join the human race.

What is actually pushing man into hell is the destructive force of sin working in him. It is his own sin, his own action that drives him away from God. God does not separate himself from man; man separates himself from God. The saying of our Lord concerning Judas points this out very forcefully: «Holy Father, keep those you have given me true to your name, so that they may be one like us. While I was with them, I kept those you had given me true to your name. I have watched over them and not one is lost except the one who chose to be lost.» (Jn 17:11, 12)

These truths are so basic, so essential to salvation, that any real progress in a retreat or in our spiritual lives as a whole depends upon their becoming real to us and their constant renewal in our hearts. The truths themselves are simple enough to state: sin makes man impotent; this means that he is powerless to help himself; only God's love can save him.

It sometimes happens in this meditation that the retreatant dwells too long on the three sins and leaves no time for the final colloquy with Christ hanging on the cross. But the colloquy is what gives meaning to the whole meditation: «Imagine Christ our Lord present before you upon the cross, and begin to speak with him, asking how it is that though He is the Creator, He has stooped to become man, and to pass from eternal life to death here in time, that thus He might die for our sins.» [53]

The question formulated here baffles understanding. How far it is beyond us! But Ignatius wants the retreatant to ask the Lord, «How is it?» What an amazing way to run a universe! God creates these little human beings and gives them freedom. Then he sends even his Son to straighten things out. Of course, it is a mystery to these poor little human creatures. Of course, they ask, «How it is that though He is the Creator, He has stooped to become man, and to pass from eternal life to death here in time, that thus he might die for our sins?»

The life of Christ, the Incarnation itself, seem at first to lead nowhere. He enters human history only to suffer on a cross and die. But notice that, throughout the «First Exercise» Christ is present. His crucified love puts the whole issue of sin into perspective. The cosmic dimension of the angels, of Adam and Eve, and of man's sin is balanced by the cosmic dimension of Christ, hanging on the cross.

We should note as well that, although Ignatius wishes this exercise to be a meditation made with the powers of memory, intellect, and will, when the exercitant begins the colloquy, he moves for a moment into Ignatian contemplation: «Imagine our Lord present before you upon the cross.» He does not listen to the Lord talking to him from the cross as he does later in the passion. Rather, he asks the Lord questions.

One reason why the colloquy does not always go well is

that the retreatant strives to keep control of his situation. His egotism gets in the way: he wants to decide the results for himself. But he is to place himself before the cross and ponder what comes. Strange as it may be, we can cling to our sense of domination even in the midst of shame and confusion for our sins; we can try to rationalize and exert our will even when faced with a mystery that overpowers us.

I think we must ponder this simple formula, «Christ died for my sins» (*cf.* Ga 2:20, 21; 1 Jn 2:2) We get so taken up by the cosmic dimension of sin and the cosmic dimension of Christ that we forget that he loved us and gave himself up for us. Karl Rahner says in his *Spiritual Exercises*[4] that even if only one man were to commit one mortal sin Christ would die on the cross for him. That is what sin means; that is the true dimension of sin. Even though there have been six billion people on the face of the earth, Christ would die for me alone.

The Lord has created man out of nothing; that is the first thing. And he has created him with a body and all his faculties; he has made him a person. Now, when he made man personal he made him a free agent, and it is this area of freedom that gives rise to the problem. For it means that he gives man responsibility.

At certain times in your life God makes his presence known to you very forcefully, as he is free to do. At other times he is «absent.» Yet he tells you to «pray always,» to continue to «Ask and you shall receive.» So there is a responsibility to prepare yourself for prayer. Here is the stunning paradox in prayer: it is a gift of God, and yet you share the responsibility for it.

Someone might feel, as I have explained the meditation, that all he has to do is to meditate on these truths and the graces will come to him. But the last phrase, «I shall ponder upon what presents itself to my mind,» indicates that what is important is not what he has figured out but how the Spirit moves him. There is a danger that he will think he is getting rational insights. This may be true, but Ignatius wants him to open up to something further in the colloquy.

Ignatius gives the lead: «Imagine Christ our Lord present before you upon the cross.» All of a sudden the personal is there; Jesus is hanging on the cross, and that changes the prayer. It is possible for us to engage in all kinds of theoretical discussions about love or about the comparisons of love. But in the colloquy the Lord is there on the cross and our prayer becomes very personal. Then, «What have I done for Christ?» is a question which involves the totality of our being — not just the intellect. «What am I doing for Christ? What ought I to do?» [53] There is a movement of my whole person and a response to Christ who has died on the cross for me.

Theology tells us that God can be hurt only in his creation. Here is where he has been hurt in his creation — in Christ hanging on the cross. This is the tremendous mystery in which God demonstrates the effect of sin and also reveals the extent of his love. Reason may help a person to appreciate Christ's death on the cross; but the person of Christ himself hanging on the cross challenges the whole man. He is not being confronted here with his own thoughts or his past life; he stands before the Lord on the cross dying for him.

The «First Exercise,» then, is an entry into the overwhelming goodness of God and the mystery of his love, his mercy, his kindness, as well as the mystery of man's helplessness and impotency arising from his own sins. He discovers not only that he needs a savior, but that he has a savior in Jesus Christ, the one his sins have crucified. And so his heart is filled with shame and confusion that he is loved in this way. At the same time, a new sense of acceptance and freedom begins to enter his being.

CHAPTER 6

PERSONAL SIN

I shall pour clean water over you and you will be cleansed; I shall cleanse you of all your defilement and all your idols. I shall give you a new heart, and put a new spirit in you; I shall remove the heart of stone from your bodies and give you a heart of flesh instead. I shall put my spirit in you, and make you keep my laws and sincerely respect my observances. You will live in the land which I gave your ancestors. You shall be my people and I will be your God. I shall rescue you from all your defilement. (Ez 36:25-29)

If our aim is to enter more deeply into the overwhelming love of God, we can face the issue of sin more calmly and more peacefully. That is certainly Ignatius's intention in the exercises of the «First Week.» Let us consider, then, the «Second Exercise,» which deals with personal sin.

Ignatius retains the composition of place given in the «First Exercise» — to view oneself as a prisoner. The retreatant is to place himself in the situation of someone chained to a chair, or compose himself in any other helpless position, in order to sense the need for a redeemer, for someone to free him. That is the attitude he takes into prayer. He asks for the grace of «a growing and intense sorrow and tears for my sins.» [55] These words again indicate an approach that is anything but rationalistic. It is a grace to experience genuine sorrow, and by the end of his thirty-day prayer the retreatant will have learned this lesson well.

How easy it is to weep buckets of tears out of discouragement with oneself, and how hard to shed tears of sorrow for one's sins. Often a man is discouraged because he has failed to live up to some ideal that he has set himself. He even grows bitter and weeps over his failures as a person. But these are not a sinner's tears for sorrow for having hurt someone whom he loves deeply.

It is possible that in his human relationships he has experienced true sorrow. It may have happened when his heart went to a person he had hurt. Then he was not concerned about the fact that *he* had committed a fault, or that *he* had committed a sin, or that *he* had hurt another, but he was concerned for someone else he had hurt, someone else he had abused. This going out of onself and this desire to heal the other person is the sorrow Ignatius means. But at that very moment the sinner experiences his inability to heal. Then true tears of sorrow can come because he cannot heal, because he can only be sorry. Only God can heal in that situation.

This divine gift of intense sorrow and tears for one's sins is itself a healing experience. Some people think that sorrow and tears are always a mark of desolation. But with regard to sin, sorrow and tears are cleansing and uplifting and redemptive. They represent the grace of truly being sorry for having offended God who is good. Of course, it is difficult to understand how a man can hurt God. God cannot be hurt in himself, but we know that, in some mysterious way, man rejects God's love when he sins. Thus, when he looks at Christ hanging on the cross, he becomes aware that in some way he hurts Christ even to the point of human death.

88

In the «Second Exercise» Ignatius moves from the conse-
quences of other people's sins to the sins of the retreatant himself. He says:

> I will call to mind all the sins of my life, reviewing year
> by year, and period by period. Three things will help me
> in this: First, to consider the place where I lived; second-
> ly, my dealings with others; thirdly, the office I have
> held. ... I will weigh the gravity of my sins, and see the
> loathsomeness and malice which every mortal sin I
> have committed has in itself, even though it were not
> forbidden. [56, 57]

The exercitant is asked to consider the real meaning of sin,
the ingratitude and the hideousness of the action that he has
performed. In other words, he is to try to understand why sin is
such a terrible thing and to experience this in the depths of his
being. He ponders the personal aspect of sin in order to grasp the
fact that sin is much more than merely breaking the law or not
living up to a set of rules. He must realize that sin has nothing
to do with the failure to live up to some image that he has of
himself. There is sin only when another person is involved. Sin
treats other persons as if they were things. Sin means that man
does not follow Paul's advice: «Always consider the other
person to be better than yourself.» (Ph 2:4)

So that a man may experience within himself the ugliness
and hatefulness of sin, Ignatius proposes a set of comparisons.
These are meant to help us appreciate the horror of sin by
contrasting it with the wonder of God's love:

> What am I compared with all men? What are all men
> compared with the angels and saints of paradise?
> Consider what all creation is in comparison with God.
> Then I alone, what can I be? I will consider all the

corruption and loathsomeness of my body. I will consider myself as a source of corruption and contagion from which has issued countless sins and evils and the most offensive poison. [58]

But consider the problem of pollution entering into small ditches and these ditches emptying into a larger ditch and then into a creek until the whole creek is polluted, then different polluted creaks polluting first a stream, next a river, and finally a lake like Lake Erie until that great body of water turns into a swamp. I guess Lake Erie is not a swamp yet, but it seems it will become one in time, if pollution is not checked.

Some image of this kind might help. For man is not merely rational: he has emotions and affections. When one starts praying about sin, it is necessary to move beyond the purely rational and pray with the whole affective side of one's being. That is the reason for this kind of imagery.

The same applies to the imagery in the meditations on the «Two Standards» and on hell. Imagery can be very helpful. Our Lord never hesitated to use it. Thus Ignatius adds a further comparison: «I will consider who God is against whom I have sinned, going through His attributes and comparing them with their contraries in me: His wisdom and my ignorance, His power with my weakness, His justice with my iniquity, His goodness with my wickedness.» [59] Such a comparison certainly belittles me and makes me experience my creaturehood and my weakness. And, with God's grace, there arises from my heart a shout of astonishment and profound love.

The retreatant has considered the disorder of sin that is present in his being independently of any decision of his own. Now in the fifth point he is concerned with his conscious acts and attitudes of refusing to love, those dimensions in his being which reject the love of God. The fifth point presents him with the amazing fact that sinful creatures are allowed to continue to exist:

> How is it that they (all creatures) have permitted me to live, and have sustained me in life! (After all, the other creatures are the instruments of God.) Why have the angels, though they are the sword of God's justice, tolerated me, guarded me, and prayed for me! Why have the saints interceded for me and asked favors for me! And the heavens, sun, moon, stars, and the elements; the fruits, birds, fishes and other animals — why have they all been at my service! [60]

Here Ignatius expresses the mystical union he sees in the cosmos between man, God, and all other creatures. All these other things are the instruments of God or expressions of God. And they are mystically united to their Maker: «How is it that the earth did not open to swallow me up, and create new hells in which I should be tormented forever!» [60] Obviously, the purpose of this kind of prayer is to come to a deep affective realization of man's sin and to perceive how unresponsive he has been in the face of so much goodness and so much love.

«I will conclude with the colloquy, extolling the mercy of God our Lord, pouring out my thoughts to Him, and giving thanks to Him that up to this very moment He has granted me life.» [61] This gift of life is given to me still, even though everything that I know about myself points the way to death. Sin points to death because sin means a rejection of that very life which God alone grants. And yet sin is man's own act. It is his personal decision to refuse God's love. Thus, the inner thrust of sin itself is towards destruction, death and hell.

The only counter-thrust is the mercy of God, the kindness of

God. *Hesed* is the Hebrew word for the tenderness, the kindness of love expressed by Hosea: «When Israel was a child I loved him, ... I myself taught Ephraim to walk, I took them in my arms; ... I led them with reins of kindness, with leading-strings of love. I was like someone who lifts an infant close against his cheek.» (Ho 11:1-4; *cf.* Ps 103:8-14) This text describes the love man has received in return for sin. Certainly it is not the way he himself would treat someone who abused him and insulted him and rejected his love. But God never gives up. Another passage in Hosea makes this point: «I will not give rein to my fierce anger, ... for I am God, not man.» (Ho 11:9; *cf.* Rm 9:15,16) In other words, where it is impossible for man to have mercy, God can have mercy, God can show kindness.

Early in the Exercises, therefore, the retreatant is face to face with this extraordinary expression of love from God, his mercy and kindness. But the experience that Ignatius wants him to achieve, I think, is a sense of joy in the possession of life, gladness over being alive. This is mentioned a number of times. He has no right to be alive, for the very thrust of sin is death. He has sinned, and yet he is alive. «Why are they dead and not me?» he asks himself in astonishment. «What is going on here? Why am I still moving around on the face of the earth? Why am I able to experience life and love?»

The «Second Exercise» is intended to bring a little more realism into his life. In fact, one of the dangers in this exercise is that he will get too involved with individual sins. But this is not the aim of this exercise. Rather, its aim is to know the mercy and love of God, to come to an awareness of God's mercy and love extended to him in the midst of his sins. I think it is also the beginning of self-understanding. In this way it points to the «Third Exercise.»

For, in the «Third Exercise» Ignatius wants the retreatant

to consider the disorder in his being. All these exercises of the «First Week» are intended to bring an appreciation of God's love in order that those who make them may become instruments of that love. To effect this, the disorders in one's life must be removed. At least, one must understand them better and begin to struggle against them.

Accordingly, the «Third Exercise» introduces us to these basic disorders. As we go through life, we can gradually perceive the direction of our failures, the repeated deviations that accumulate into a pattern. Beneath the surface of our external actions we should be able to discern the more basic sources of disorder. This is worth knowing about because the grace of God will be available to us in our yearnings for what is better.

The grace to be sought remains unchanged. Now, it should be remarked that to achieve not only sorrow but also *tears* for sin may depend on the ordinary range of an individual's affective life. In what ways do you usually express your feelings? Some people almost never give way to tears, but you have only to *look* at others for tears to start. In certain cases you merely ask, «Don't you know that God loves you?» and the tears flow freely.

If I may speak of men rather than women, it is an interesting fact that most men are so stolid and unemotional that they rarely weep in front of others. They may act differently at a sentimental movie where nobody can see them. Then there can be lots of tears. Most men, especially Anglo-Saxons, feel it is unmanly to cry. So I always say, if you cannot pray for exterior tears, then pray for interior tears. Your relationship to God and to Christ our Lord ought to emerge from your deepest self. In certain individuals it may not matter that external tears do not come, as long as their whole being is involved in the movement of sorrow for sin.

There are tears of joy as well as tears of sorrow. People's eyes will often fill with tears on meeting a friend they have not seen for years. When someone is trying to express gratitude he may not say anything: he may only grasp your hand. When there is deep appreciation or thankfulness, a look at the person's eyes will reveal his interior attitude.

For all these reasons, what Ignatius says about tears should perhaps be understood in a relative sense: the exact forms of *external* expression may vary a good deal from one person to another. But the deeper reality of sorrow, the full intensity of sorrow, which can be manifested in many different ways, is the principal aim to be sought. And in every case, whatever the particular manner of expression that suits the individual, each one's affective life, his whole self and not merely a part of him, must become involved in his relationship with the forgiving God.

But it is important to remember in all the meditations on sin that the retreatant is not merely looking at himself and his depressing failures but concentrating more emphatically on the amazing reality of God's love. The image of the Good Shepherd going out to get the lost sheep is a good one. If you were the shepherd in charge of a hundred sheep, and one of them became stuck in the brambles at the end of a tiring day, I suspect you would probably kick it home. But the Good Shepherd puts the sheep on his shoulders and carries the lost one home.

Ignatius uses the term «mortal sin.» Many pages have been written in the last ten years on mortal sin and the «fundamental option.» The latter is the ability of man to give himself totally to the Lord or to evil. One decision that could affect the fundamental option is the marriage choice, the giving of oneself totally to another person. The opposite, an act of adultery, could also involve a fundamental option. To kill a man intentionally would bring the fundamental option into play. Besides homicide and adultery, the third sin given serious attention in the early Church was apostasy, the denial of one's faith.

What is normally called «mortal sin» might better be termed «serious sin.» It is the kind of sin which could, when certain conditions were fulfilled, mean that a person's deepest self had turned away from God. It could be as serious as that. There are also venial sins and imperfections. All of these, however you list them, have one thing in common — disorder. A person has given in to this disorder, or he has promoted the disorder in his life, or he has not responded to grace.

The intensity of the love relationship with God will indicate to the person the degree of his sin. In a love relationship between a man and a woman, what would be considered a very slight action in one set of circumstances might be considered a great offense in another. The seriousness of the offense depends on the quality or intensity of the love that is shared. But the common dimension we are speaking about in both cases is the basic element of disorder and ingratitude.

I think the difference is expressed in the words «deep-felt.» Obviously, you can have surface feelings and you can have deep feelings. There are different levels of feeling, and such feeling is sometimes connected with the emotions and sometimes not. In some instances a felt experience can overflow emotionally in tears, for example. Maybe some of you have experienced tears that were very quiet while your whole being was at rest. It is a time of quiet appreciation when your whole being overflows. It is a quiet thing, a peaceful thing. At other times there might be deep sobbing. The tears do not tell anything. What is significant is why they come, from whom they come, and where they are leading. What is the interior experience accompanying the tears? The same is true of blushing. You may blush from embarrassment, or from excitement, or gratitude.

When Ignatius describes consolation, he speaks about intense love for the Creator. This is something a person feels with his whole being. Whether there is an emotional overflow is another question. But tears are healing when they are the affective response to grace. When the person experiences this deep-felt knowledge of Christ, then tears indicate that the totality of his being is responding.

The subject of tears and one's affective response in prayer leads me to speak about three kinds of love. The first is affected love. This is not love at all, because it is only the appearance of love. No actions accompany affected love. Next, there is effective love. This is the love that shows itself in action. Finally, there is constant love. Constant love is the abiding love for a person. Like a mother's love for her child, it is there now and it will always be there.

An example of constant love that might help is the attitude of a mother to her child when he comes running into the house with dirty shoes and dirty face and dirty clothes. The mother sees a mess all over her clean floor. She becomes quite provoked. She gives the child a couple of good slaps, and only then does she discover that his finger is bleeding. What a change! But this is how constant love behaves. It can be seen as well in the kind of love of a woman whose lover is fighting in a war. She is present with her man all the time he is away.

As we discuss the *Exercises* some may feel that in their retreat they did not dwell on many of the points Ignatius gives. Have they really made the Exercises? The Lord would probably answer: «Only one thing is necessary.» Ignatius gives many points — all of them intended to help the retreatant meet the Lord. It would be surprising if every individual found him everywhere. After all, Jesus Christ adapts himself in a unique way to each person whom he calls. The right question, then, would be, «In my particular case — where did I find the Lord?» Or better still, «Where did the Lord find me?» When you know what points were special for you, you should concentrate on them. In fact, that advice holds good for all four «Weeks» of the Exercises.

Speaking of repetition in the «Third Exercise,» Ignatius says: «In doing this, we should pay attention to and dwell upon those points in which we have experienced greater consolation or desolation or greater spiritual appreciation.» [62] It is very possible that a retreatant might not get beyond the first line of the «Principle and Foundation» or beyond the first point of the «Second Exercise.» But that is all he may need to make the colloquy. In fact, it is often better if he does not get through all five points.

To receive a genuinely deep consolation Abraham Maslow would call a «peak experience.» [5] But peak experiences go both ways: there are the ones that exalt and there are the others that depress. Ignatius instructs the exercitant to go back over the matter or the thoughts in which he found consolation. Most find this easy to do. But he is also advised to return to whatever caused desolation, and that may be much more difficult to do.

For example, he might find it difficult to consider Ignatius's comparisons: «His wisdom with my ignorance, his power with my weakness, etc.» Nevertheless, he ought to keep going back to it. One man to whom I was giving a retreat said he found repetitions like physical exercise. If one muscle is not working well, you keep working and working it, exercising it to make it supple, so it will work properly.

Sometimes a person finds it truly difficult to accept the fact that he has sinned. He needs to discover the reason for this. What is behind his reluctance? Why is this human fact of sin so difficult to accept when the whole gospel is filled with evidence that Christ came to die for sinners? Why should it depress the person?

The basic strategy of the Exercises, beginning with the «Third Exercise» is to keep going back to what is difficult or to what is consoling, and in this repetition to go deeper and deeper and deeper into the prayer experience. Thus, in the «First Week» there should be a return to the experience of desolation until one receives a deep knowledge of his sins and a feeling of abhorrence for them. Eventually an understanding of the disorder of his actions will be gained. This is the purpose of the repetition, and the director will usually insist that a retreatant make a number of repetitions, especially if he thinks he has «got it made» the first time.

In the «Third Exercise» the exercitant delves deeply into the root cause of his sins, not just to gain sorrow for the actions that he performed, but to find out why he performed them. Most experience the syndrome, sin-resolution-sin-resolution, even though each repentance is accompanied by great sorrow and tears and confession. This should make him aware of the need to find the root cause.

The resolution to abandon one's sin is important, but it is only one part of the exercise. The retreatant usually wishes to overcome his sinful tendency altogether, to stop it before it gets moving. That is the reason for a deeper investigation. And that is why I said it is better to obtain a knowledge of one's basic disorder than to run through the list of sins that he faces in the «Second Exercise.»

What is salutary in this exercise is the realization that «I cannot do it alone.» It is so difficult for me that I need our Lady — it is always good to start with her. And in this exercise, the «Triple Colloquy» introduces the cosmic dimension again, for our Lady is the personification of the Church, the believing body that is operating in this cosmos. She is not the personification of humanity — we would say that Christ performs that role. Thus, the prayer moves one from the believing body to Christ, and from Christ to the Father. This suggests how difficult this exercise can be and how important it is for me to find the thrust in my life that causes me to sin constantly.

The «Fourth Exercise» is styled a «summary.» It is a review of all of the matter in the three foregoing exercises by taking up again all that has already been gone through on the history of sin and on personal sin. It differs from the repetition in that one does not dwell only on the points where greater consolation or desolation was experienced. Rather, it changes the perspective by affording an overall view of what has been experienced in prayer.

The points of deeper consolation and desolation will normally stand out in the memory, but they will be set in the larger framework and will gain in clarity and value from the freshness of approach. The summary should help to impress the ideas more deeply on the mind, especially if they are resumed with the diligence and concentration which Ignatius recommends. The exercise concludes with the same «Triple Colloquy» as does the «Third Exercise.» The retreatant has to attain an awareness of his helplessness which will move him to seek help from our Lady, our Lord, and the Father. It is the desire of union with Mary, Jesus and the Father that is urging him to investigate himself, even though the task is a difficult one.

A helpful subject of meditation is Ezekiel's allegory of Israel as the woman who took to herself all the gifts that had been given to her by the Lord, instead of returning them to him. (Ezk 16:1-63) A deep understanding of sin and disorder can be found more easily in the smaller events of life. Most people do not commit many terrible sins like adultery, murder, or apostasy, but they do perform a large number of small acts that tie them down like Gulliver. The venial sins a man commits, the imperfections that run through his life, make him faint-hearted in his vocation and destroy the magnanimity of his offering. His generosity goes, and, before he knows it, he has fallen into the habit of expecting very little of God. The investigation of little things, therefore, will often point to the more basic disorder in one's being.

Sometimes another person may be the direct messenger of this grace, as was Nathan to David. It was the prophet who was able to point out to David the terrible direction of his sin. How human was David in his blindness, indignant that the rich man should take a little ewe lamb from the poor man but blind to his own crime! (2 S 11:1 — 12:14) As directors, you will often see a person's delusions or failings more clearly than he does because you are standing outside him. It becomes your job to lead that person to the interior knowledge of himself, but not too forcefully or too pointedly. You want him to come to that realization through the Spirit acting in him.

How does one find the basic disorder? Sometimes by looking at one's talents. For quite often we discover that our basic disorder is just the opposite of our basic virtue. The saying, «generous to a fault,» expresses the awareness that a person's vices are related to his virtue. It is important then to look at both sides of our behavior, at the totality of our acts and responses.

My experience is that, as the person is meditating or praying, there will be experiences of disquiet or anxiety and fear, experiences of desolation. If you encourage the person to trace these down, he will usually discover the basic disorder operating in him. Maybe it is the desire to be accepted. Maybe it is the fear of failure. As he keeps praying, the basic disorder becomes more and more clearly defined.

This investigation works together with sorrow and contrition for one's sins to form a purpose of amendment. Thus, a person may come to the awareness: «My basic disorder is anger, and I have to be very careful of anger.» But perhaps it is only in the «Second or Third Week» of the Exercises that the person will discover that the anger in him is due to a specific cause and is expressed in particular circumstances. He will learn to be very careful in those situations and to pray for a greater awareness of how much God loves him. Usually most basic disorders are connected with a lack of awareness of God's love.

The realization of the basic fault depends on an attitude of openness in the individual who is looking for help. The director can ask a lot of questions in order to discover the right matter for prayer.

There are many reasons for searching out one's basic disorder. The first is to increase one's ability to love. The second is to help avoid serious sins and a total rejection of God through the fundamental option. Not many individual sins but the final acquiescence in the basic disorder will constitute the fundamental option against the Lord.

The «Fifth Exercise» is on hell. One question that arises here concerns the method of prayer. Ignatius calls it «a meditation on hell.» In the «Second Week» a similar method of prayer is called an «Application of the Senses.» The difference seems to be that now the five senses are to be applied imaginatively to the truth of hell — whence it is called a «meditation.» But in the «Second Week» the senses are applied not to a truth of faith, but to the persons present in the revealed mysteries of our Lord's life.

Once again, the purpose of the hell meditation is to move the retreatant out of himself so that he may experience the destructive force of sin as it works to destroy him. Ignatius tells him to «ask for what I desire. Here it will be to beg for a deep sense of the pain which the lost suffer, that if because of my faults I forget the love of the eternal Lord, at least the fear of these punishments will keep me from falling into sin.» [65] The purpose of this exercise is to keep one from sinning, that is, from rejecting the love of the Lord.

This meditation on hell directs man outside himself to God. It is true he is fearful of punishment, but he is more concerned lest he offend against the love of the eternal Lord. On one side, the inner dynamic of sin will separate him forever from the Lord who loves him. And, if nothing else will work, maybe this negative side, his fear of punishment, will be effective.

Ignatius gives a rather baroque picture of hell, as in Dante's *Inferno*. One of the ways I suggest that people make this meditation is in terms of the psyche. Men are psychosomatic beings. Their interior state influences the body. Thus, he may start with the basic experience of hell, which is separation from God, separation from the one who loves him and from the one who knows him best. If he starts with this experience of separation and dwells on it at the level of sensation, then this meditation may be more efficacious.

What does he see if he considers himself separated from God? What is going to be the psychosomatic reaction in his eyes, in his ears, in his nostrils, in his touch? By means of this method, his whole self may enter into the experience of separation. It is not merely an intellectual apprehension that «I'll be separated from God» but an experience of ultimate loss affecting his whole being. Again our goal is deep-felt experience.

We cannot say that on the cross Christ suffered the pains of the damned. But he recites the opening verse of a Psalm: «My God, my God, why have you deserted me?» (Mt 27:46;

Ps 22:1) — which reveals the pain of separation he was experiencing. The Psalm goes on to express union with God and the desire to praise God's name in the assembly. But Christ's recitation of the psalm indicates his own vivid experience of abandonment.

Exactly what that is, we do not know. But since the retreatant is seeking a true understanding of sin and its effect on him, he has to be aware that it means a similar separation from the one who created him and who is the ground of his being. If he starts with this notion of separation and lets it move into his different senses, I think he will achieve the purpose of this exercise. The colloquy at the end of the exercise may be a very personal one. He gives thanks to God our Lord for not putting an end to his life nor permitting him to fall into self-destruction. [*cf.* 71] He is overwhelmed to know that he is still alive, even though he does not deserve to be. Someone might say, «Up to this point I have committed sins here and here and here. But in each instance the Lord has forgiven me. So what is the danger?» The danger is that one's basic disorder will actually overwhelm him and drag him into hell. The retreatant considers that possibility and enters into it. He tries to experience what sin truly is by meditating on hell. At the end he makes a fervent act of gratitude to the Lord that sin has not yet driven him to that terrible destiny.

It is a controversial point whether these five exercises should be given on a single day or not. One variation is to give the exercise on hell on the very first day: the purpose is to instill in the retreatant a profound sense of God's mercy from the start. Then this exercise may only be a consideration of our Lord's parable of Dives in hell. (Lk 16:19-31) Again, some directors move the «Third Exercise» and the repetitions to the final day or days of the «First Week» as means to the three graces which by then the retreatant is very anxious to obtain.

Ignatius adds further alternatives in the «Annotations»:

One who is educated or talented, but engaged in public affairs or necessary business, should take an hour and a half daily for the Spiritual Exercises.

First, the end for which man is created should be explained to him, then for half an hour the Particular Examination of Conscience may be presented, then the General Examination of Conscience and the method of confessing and of receiving Holy Communion.

For three days, let him meditate each morning for an hour on the first, second and third sins. [19]

Outside the thirty-day retreat experience, then, Ignatius suggests that a retreatant can repeat the «First Exercise» three times; next, the one on personal sin can be made three times; then, the one on the punishment due to sin, which is hell. There is an advantage to giving the «First, Second and Fifth Exercises» on the one day in that this experience of the whole dynamic of sin gives an incentive for the three graces of the «Third Exercise.»

At the end of the exercises of the «First Week,» Ignatius indicates the possibility of introducing other exercises on such subjects as death and judgment. [71] I use them in order to give some variety in prayer, when that seems necessary. But the basic graces to be sought are the same — sorrow, contrition, abhorrence of sin, knowledge of the world, and knowledge of one's own disorder. These exercises on death and judgment can give an existential awareness of creaturehood and sinfulness. They increase the retreatant's sense of reality.

The question of death is something which, sooner or later,

the retreatant has to face. In fact, there are three places in the Exercises where he meditates on death. This additional exercise is one place; the others occur during the passion and resurrection. There are two ways to approach death, either in terms of judgment or in terms of salvation and Christ's triumph.

Finally, what the retreatant seeks in these exercises are graces — free gifts from God. Of course, he can confidently expect that graces will be given during the Exercises. Scripture indicates that the Lord desires to give and to give more than the retreatant desires to receive. (*cf.* Rm 8:26; Ep 3:20) Both the one making the Exercises and the director himself need faith in the Lord's willingness to give grace. But much patience is needed; both must wait upon the Lord. Often he does not give precisely the kind of grace requested, nor at the exact time it is sought.

The words of St. Paul express very succinctly the sentiments of the exercises of the «First Week»: «Who will rescue me from this body doomed to death? Thanks be to God through Jesus Christ our Lord!» (Rm 7:24) Through prayer man has entered into the destructive force of sin and disorder that drive towards death and hell. He has also experienced his own ingratitude to the personal love of the Trinity for him, and he is filled with shame, confusion, sorrow and tears. His sin and disorder belong to the interpersonal order; they are directed, not merely against himself, but also against God. And his prayer has made him aware of his helplessness and impotency in the face of these self-centered destructive forces. So he cries out in amazement that he has a savior, Jesus Christ, and that he is still alive, sustained by the savior's love. He is also conscious that he will always need the freeing action of divine grace, and his hope is that the Spirit within him will never let him forget his need.

CHAPTER 7

THE KINGDOM OF CHRIST

Now he was standing one day by the Lake of Gennesaret, with the crowd pressing round him listening to the word of God, when he caught sight of two boats close to the bank. The fishermen had gone out of them and were washing their nets. He got into one of the boats — it was Simon's — and asked him to put out a little from the shore. Then he sat down and taught the crowds from the boat.

When he had finished speaking he said to Simon, 'Put out into deep water and pay out your nets for a catch.' 'Master,' Simon replied, 'we worked hard all night long and caught nothing, but if you say so, I will pay out the nets.' And when they had done this they netted such a huge number of fish that their nets began to tear, so they signalled to their companions in the other boats to come and help them; when these came, they filled the two boats to sinking point.

When Simon Peter saw this he fell at the knees of Jesus saying, 'Leave me, Lord; I am a sinful man'. For he and all his companions were completely overcome by the catch they had made; so also were James and John, sons of Zebedee, who were Simon's partners. But Jesus said to Simon, 'Do not be afraid; from now on it is men you will catch'. Then, bringing their boats back to land, they left everything and followed him. (Lk 5:1-11)

The call of the apostles provides an excellent context

for discussing the «Call of the King.» Here Peter is conscious, as the retreatant becomes in the «First Week», that before God he is a sinner. And yet he is called by the very Lord he has sinned against! To know that one has received a call is almost the ideal experience of grace — of receiving a personal gift that one could never possibly deserve. It will help us to understand the special role of this meditation if we review for a moment the sequence of graces, the unearned gifts, that the Exercises bring to our awareness.

In our culture, from earliest childhood we too easily come to know sin either in a very guilt-ridden, negative way or in an external, legalistic manner characterized by the admonition, «Thou shalt not.» As a result, we can miss the true significance of sin: it is what reduces man to a state of helplessness and impotence more dire than anything arising out of creaturehood alone. Creaturehood and contingency limit man to living from moment to moment in constant dependence upon a power outside himself. But sin makes him truly impotent, truly helpless to receive and return love. One purpose of the «First Week» is to come to this consciousness. It is true that the retreatant needs as well an awareness of sorrow and fear because he has offended God who is good. But it is when he feels helpless and impotent that he begins to experience the reality and meaning of grace.

Grace creates a whole new order of things. It is not just a continuation of the first creative act of God; rather, it builds a new relationship. The relationship with God is totally new because it is interpersonal. When God forgives, he gives his own person. Maybe the analogy of a man walking down a crowded city street may help. He is alone and these beings around him are all strangers. Then he sees someone he loves coming towards him, and suddenly his life moves onto a new plateau. Even to know this much about our relationship with God is a grace, but to experience it is a grace of world-shaking dimensions. By the end of the «First Week,» therefore, the retreatant should resemble the sinful woman in Luke's gospel who washes the Lord's feet. (Lk 7:36-50) The Lord is, after all, her savior. He is the one who lifts her out of her helplessness and impotency. He loves her and bestows on her the ability to love.

Like the sinful woman, the retreatant experiences a deep sense of relief. He is lifted up, because in the poverty of his creaturehood and sinfulness he knows that he is safe and strong in God's hands. What happens through the grace of the Lord in the «First Week» is that he becomes conscious that he can do all things in God who strengthens him. (*cf*. Ph 4:13)

This experience of grace is taken for granted by Ignatius, I think, as our essential preparation for the «Kingdom» meditation. Throughout the preceding days, the exercitant has received many expressions of God's merciful love for him. In pondering the «Principle and Foundation» he renewed his awareness of the love God showered on him as his Creator. He later came to see that only a special love could have sustained his existence in a universe disordered by fallen angels and by sinful Adam and Eve. Furthermore, God's love kept him alive even when he freely chose to allow the disorders of sin to take root in his inmost heart.

Even today God does not let him die, does not permit the ravages of sin to reach their completion in death and in the total separation of hell. In creating man God set in motion forces which sustain him. But once man becomes involved in sin, destructive forces assert themselves. To save him from the inexorable destruction his sin has unleashed, only an extraordinary intervention of God's love will suffice.

In the «First Week,» then he has relived that extraordinary love that lifts him out of his state of helplessness: «We were still helpless when at his appointed moment Christ died for sinful men. It is not easy to die even for a good man — though of course for someone really worthy, a man might be prepared to die — but what proves that God loves us is that Christ died for us while we were still sinners.» (Rm 5:6-8)

In the «Kingdom» the retreatant suddenly advances to a new awareness — that Christ is calling him to assist in the work of redemption. It would be comfortable for him simply to bask in the presence of the merciful God. But the Lord comes with his grace to expand a man's heart and to give him the desire and generosity to do something about this disordered universe. God moves into the very freedom that is destroying itself in the pursuit of sin and calls it forth to the service of love. All at once a man recognizes the personal presence of God. And with the self-knowledge of the «First Week,» he truly understands the prayer of St. Francis, «Make me a channel of your peace.»

Through prayer man becomes conscious of the weakness in his sinful nature and of his dependence on Christ for a life of freedom. Christ's human nature is like his own but without the self-inflicted wounds of sin. Christ's nature became the instrument of the Trinity's redemptive act. It is the instrument by which Christ overcame sin and death. It was his personal relationship with the Father which enabled his weak human nature to achieve man's redemption. And he is inviting individual men and women to unite themselves with him and to help bring about the salvation of the world.

What an extraordinary invitation! The retreatant is moved to another experience of grace, another expression of God's love. He is being called to work with Christ in overcoming the disorder that is in the universe and that is in himself. How amazing this is when one thinks about it. He needs God's sustaining love not only to keep him in being but to prevent him from sinning. But Christ invites him to help redeem others.

This call of Christ to man is like the call to Peter. And Peter's reaction is understandable: «Depart from me, Lord, I am a sinful man.» He has just witnessed Christ's miraculous power and is stunned by Christ's invitation to follow him. The retreatant's first response can resemble Peter's «What does he need me for?»

What is overlooked in the initial surprise is that the «Call of the King» brings with it further gifts — a soul-expanding generosity, new, burning desires for service, a remarkable confidence in what the Lord can do. Jesus Christ, the Son of God, offers him the chance to work at his side. How can he refuse? On another occasion the Lord asked his apostles: «'Do you want to go away too?' Simon Peter answered, 'Lord, who shall we go to? You have the message of eternal life.'»(Jn 6:67-8) Christ wants Peter's boat, Peter's nets, Peter's work, and Peter himself.

The Lord does not merely want to save the individual man but at the same time to enlist him in the struggle to save the world. The character of God's saving action is different from what we might expect. Not only does he forgive man but he wants to share his own life with man by including him in his labors and his loving acts for others. Since these truths cannot be absorbed by the retreatant all at once, it was the practice of Ignatius to give this «Kingdom» meditation on the repose day, with a repetition in the evening. Throughout the day the exercitant has time to take it in.

His difficulties should not be minimized. His ordinary veil of vanity and pride has been torn away to reveal to his unsuspecting gaze the deep-rooted disorders and sinfulness in his life. How could he, of all people, he wonders, be called to labor with the Son of God? What he fails to realize is that he is called to labor with Jesus Christ who is himself weak and humiliated.

110

As he told his apostles: «How happy are the poor in spirit,» (Mt 5:3) — that is, how happy are those who feel the need of God.

«Mine is not a kingdom of this world,» he said to Pilate. (Jn 18:36) His kingdom is not founded upon worldly calculations, is not established by means of earthly power, nor does it survive through secular wisdom. It is based on dependence, his personal dependence on the will of his loving Father. St. Paul expresses this weakness of Christ in a startling way: «For our sake God made the sinless one into sin.» (2 Co 5:21) Moreover, only in our very weakness can the victory of Christ over sin and death express itself. For, Jesus does in fact come to us in our weakness, as Paul says,«For it is when I am weak that I am strong.» (2 Co 12:10) and it was «to shame what is strong that God chose what is weak.» (1 Co 1:27)

As a stimulus to our generosity, the meditation opens with the parable of a call made by an earthly king. It evokes the spontaneous generosity that a man or a woman would feel toward a good human leader. It enables our innately generous nature to reach out beyond the confines of our usual self-preoccupation. The apostolic urges and desires conferred on every Christian at baptism are now given a real opportunity to come into play. Enthusiasm for the inspiring lives of the saints kindles in our hearts.

At certain moments in our lives we have known what it means to be generous, to work unselfishly for others. We may even have a picture of ourselves serving Jesus Christ that is unique to ourselves and our times. These may re-enter our minds at this time, even in the form of somewhat romantic longings. In the early life of Ignatius, we may recall, he gave himself up to ambitious day-dreams, yearning to emulate the deeds of Benedict, of Francis, and of Dominic. The call of the earthly king is calculated to prepare the retreatant for the call of the eternal king. The eternal king is the risen Christ speaking to him, the

Christ of the resurrection who will be with him all the way through to the «Contemplation to Attain Love of God.»

This meditation is more difficult today because of the word «king.» In order to appreciate why the call of a king can have special meaning, it may help to know something about the ideal of kingship. Even though many men who bore the title abused it badly, the ideal itself has been very influential in the history of our civilization. After all, the Church herself celebrates the feast of Christ the King.

The significance of a king is quite different from that of an ordinary leader. It has a dimension to it that makes it unique. Napoleon wanted to be made king because he knew that the kingly mystique extended beyond that of a military dictator. The king signifies much more than president or prime minister.

In Shakespeare's play, *Anthony and Cleopatra,* Anthony refers to Cleopatra as «Egypt.» This means that Cleopatra carries in her person the whole country that is Egypt. She is not just the leader of the Egyptians; somehow she *is* Egypt. In the same way, King David is somehow «Israel.» The king personifies in himself and carries in himself the whole nation. At one time, as you may know, if you killed the king, you won the war. It did not matter whether his troops were winning the battle or not. This, then, is the point for us; in a marvelous and unique way, Christ is king and lord of the universe. Scripture even calls him the Last Adam and head of the human race. This is the special significance of the word «king,» but despite all that has been said, the concept itself may be considered secondary in this meditation.

What is crucial in the meditation is to grasp how a human leader can attract people to him and inspire them to be generous, even to the point of giving their lives for a cause. Such a leader usually arrives on the scene during an economic depression or some other state of national weakness or helplessness. He is able to appeal to the people as a savior and to tell them what needs to be done. Hitler did this with the German people. Mussolini and Castro did it too.

Castro is a very interesting example. At the time of his emergence as a leader, Cuba was under the heel of Battista, a powerful dictator. The country was in a bad way because a small group of plutocrats were exploiting the people. Castro said he could correct this sad condition. He presented his plan to the people. When the fighting started, he went into the hills and eager partisans followed. They lived the rugged, rough, guerilla life with him. But he was there in their midst, fighting at their side, until they overcame the dictator.

Another example is Churchill, who said to the people, «All I have to promise you is blood, sweat, and tears.» He was a man who knew how to arouse the generosity of people to sacrifice. There have been other men gifted with the same charisma: Pope John XXIII, for example, and John F. Kennedy who said, «Don't ask what your country can do for you; ask what you can do for your country.» There have been women leaders as well: St. Teresa of Avila, St. Catherine of Sienna, Sister Kenny, Coretta King, Mother Teresa of Calcutta, and the foundresses of religious orders.

For religious or those considering a religious life, the lives of the saints, especially of the founder or foundress, can be very helpful. Because the sense of identity can become very strong, the desire to work with them and be like them wells up in members of the order. «The love of Christ urges us on.»

There are men like this today. When they meet you and talk to you, it is very difficult to turn away from them or their work. In fact, if there is any generosity in your heart at all, you long to work with them. This natural inclination to be generous and throw oneself into a cause is used by Ignatius to set the tone of the meditation. It is an aid to lift a person out of himself, as a preparation for the call of Christ the King.

When the retreatant turns to the call of Christ, these desires to live and work with the King are that much stronger. The experience of being loved by the Lord, still powerfully in his heart from the exercises of the «First Week,» urges him to respond. But, I suppose, this meditation gives the opportunity for his true self, united with the indwelling Spirit, to respond and identify with Jesus Christ. It is another instance where he can cry out in the Spirit, «*Abba,* Father,» together with Jesus.

It is important to realize the personal dimension in this meditation. The person of Jesus is inviting me. It is not some ideal, some platonic image, that I am going to follow, but a live human being. Nor does this exercise seek to perpetuate Christ's «spirit» in the sense that one would speak of the «spirit» of John F. Kennedy or Pope John XXIII. It is not the spirit, or the plan, or the ambition of a dead man that is remembered here, but a living person who is present and calls me now. Christ is risen and is living permanently in history. He has not changed, but he is changing everything into himself. Thus, the meditation of the «Kingdom» centers on the resurrected Christ.

Prayer upon this personal summons from the Lord can be an effective instrument in spiritual direction. If you wish to find out what kind of generosity a person has, you might present him with this meditation. Or you might use Scripture passages that will do the same thing as the «Call of the King.» (*cf.* Jn 10:1-18; 1 Co 1:26-31; Ph 3:7-14) Is he unable to commit himself to a cause or to a person? Is he too lethargic, or without incentive? Or is he too afraid? Here again the director may see the dimension of fear or anxiety in the face of responsibility. If that is the case, he may be able to help the person with his vocation. With the help of this meditation the person should grow in knowledge of himself and should appreciate more fully that the «weak things of the world has God chosen to confound the strong.» (1 Co 1:27)

Because it has application to the eternal Lord, the retreatant should not skip over the appeal placed by Ignatius in the mouth of the human leader: «Therefore, whoever wishes to join with me in this enterprise must be content with the same food, drink, clothing, etc. as mine. So, too, he must work with me by day, and watch with me by night, etc., that as he has had a share in the toil with me, afterwards, he may share in the victory with me.» [93] These words spoken by the earthly king are important, even though Christ's call is expressed a little differently.

And the response to the earthly king is also significant for our response to Christ's call, although the phrasing is slightly altered here as well: «Consider what the answer of good subjects ought to be to a king so generous and noble-minded, and consequently, if anyone would refuse the invitation of such a king, how justly he would deserve to be condemned by the whole world, and looked upon as an ignoble knight.» [94] Ignatius wants us to apply these words to Christ our Lord.

In the «Call of an Earthly King» the first appeal is made to the work he wants to do. But how much more worthy of consideration is the work of Christ the eternal King! «To all His summons goes forth, and to each one in particular He addresses the words: 'It is my will to conquer the whole world and all my enemies, and thus to enter into the glory of my Father.'» [95] The imagery here is military, but when Christ conquers the whole world and all his enemies, he converts them to himself. The conquering of Christ's enemies means that they become aware how much God loves them. When Ignatius says, «how much more worthy of consideration is Christ our Lord, the Eter-

115

nal King, before whom is assembled the whole world,» [95] he is speaking, of course, of the character of Jesus. What a beautiful person he is! The appeal of his person in faith precedes what he asks us to do. But the Lord's work is also beautiful. It is the most important work a human being can undertake — to be with Christ in bringing about the salvation of the world.

One becomes conscious of this in a hospital at the bedside of people who are dying. They know they are dying. They have lost interest in seeing a doctor. They want to see a person of faith — not necessarily a priest, but a person of faith, a person who really believes in the resurrection. Is death the end or not? That is what they want to know.

And they want to know about the love of Christ, and his triumph over sin and death. Quite apart from the moment of death, this does become the basic issue for people. The awareness that there is a God of love in this world that looks so topsy-turvy can be a powerful force in the lives of men. There is a great need to tell them about God's love so that they can love other people, since God is the source of love.

In the «Kingdom» meditation our Lord goes on: «Therefore, whoever wishes to join me in this enterprise must be willing to labor with me, that by following me in suffering, he may follow me in glory.» [95] Here Christ reveals another characteristic of a great leader: he insists on being with his men. He is right beside them; he is leading them. He is not behind them, pushing them forward.

They tell a story of Napoleon's way of dealing with one of his generals who was having trouble with his troops. The troops did not show much courage or initiative. Napoleon placed a piece of string on a table and asked the general to push the piece of string across the table. The general tried but without success. Then, Napoleon asked him to pull it across. A good example of leadership. In the same way, Christ is with the Christian in the midst of the struggle.

Ignatius is very insistent about our unity with Jesus and his sharing of his work, his pains, his victory with us. Thus, the first clause, «whoever wishes to join me in this enterprise must be willing to labor with me,» is balanced by the second, «that by following me in suffering he may also follow me in glory.» Our companionship with Jesus cannot be overstressed. The Emmanuel theme in our apostolic work is part of Christ's call. As he says in the Apocalypse: «You see this city? Here God lives among men. He will make *his home among them; they shall be his people,* and he will be their God; his name is *God-with-them.* He will wipe away all tears from their eyes.» (Rv 21:3-4)

The second point contains a startling expression: «Consider that all persons who have judgment and reason will offer themselves entirely for this work.» [96] This sounds as if my response is to come through reason and judgment rather than from a temporary burst of enthusiasm. Deep conviction ought to be the reason why I offer myself entirely for this work.

It should be noted that the «Call of the King» does not involve the choice of a way of life. It is intended to stir up generosity and an awareness of Christ's call — immediately after the meditation on sin and on the Lord's merciful and saving love. It involves an offering of myself to work with him. Obviously, my ability to give myself totally to the Lord in great generosity could only be a gift of his love. His grace alone could achieve it.

But Ignatius presents this consideration much in the same way as he presented the «Principle and Foundation»: «Man is created to praise, reverence, and serve God our Lord, and by this means to save his soul.» [23] The retreatant has just discovered in the last week that he does not save his own soul; God saves it. And God is his savior; Jesus alone is his savior, and he himself is impotent. And yet the «Principle and Foundation» was presented as though he were going to save his soul by himself.

Similarly, the «Kingdom» is presented as though he were going to make a generous response on his own. Now, he knows that this is the response he should make, but he is conscious he cannot make it by himself. Just as the call of Christ is a grace, his response can only be a grace. Grace is always free as is the call of Christ. Every Christian is freely invited in this way.

Moreover, humanly speaking, he should respond. His intellect tells him that he should respond. He is aware that, if he does not respond to such a call, there is something really wrong. I think the element of amazement and gratitude at being called by one so good and for so worthy a cause is behind Ignatius's admonition that anyone who refused «would deserve to be condemned.»

He is invited to follow Christ as a Christian. He cannot refuse, without sinning, to live up to his baptismal commitment. But sin is not in question in this meditation. Within the baptismal commitment one is free to follow one vocation or another. There is no sin directly involved in not following a state of life one may feel called to. And the «kingdom» meditation is intended merely to instill generosity and openness to the Lord's will.

What has preceded this meditation are the many experiences of God's love and mercy. Within that context, how could anyone possibly think of refusing the invitation? Christ has lifted me out of the mire, out of my helplessness. Now he asks me to serve with him and work with him. The figure of leader or king is only meant to introduce the personal invitation of his call. Maybe another image of Christ, summing-up my total relationship with him, will emerge as he calls me to respond totally.

The basic point of the exercise, as far as I can see, is the generous response to love offered. It is Christ offering his love, but offering it in a new way. He is saying, «Come and labor with me.» It is the offering of companionship. The prayer at the end indicates the kind of generosity needed to labor with Christ. It is a response in love and generosity to live as Christ lives.

Furthermore, no man could deserve this call: it is a privilege that Christ is giving him. Christ invites him to be with himself, and his reaction must not be a craven refusal or fearful neutrality, but a response of joy mingled with surprise: «Me? — Are you calling even me? Yes! I'll come!» The reaction should be one of generosity and astonishment that Christ is asking him to do this, rather than one of fear that he is going to make him work hard or suffer. That is why the meditation is so crucial in the Exercises and why it is important when you are giving spiritual direction. What is the reaction of the counselee? Is it a reaction of fear at this invitation, or is it a reaction of surprise, of one overwhelmed that Christ should ask?

To what extent the director should spell out the meaning of this meditation — along the lines I have suggested above — is a difficult question. The same question arises in other exercises and for other ascetical principles of the spiritual life. Grace is a subtle thing. It does not overpower man's freedom. Perhaps Ignatius presents the meditations as briefly as he does in order to leave grace free to operate. If the whole meditation is explained by the director, the retreatant might go back to his room and be content to bask in the explanations the director has given. Besides, the director wants to see how the retreatant reacts to the meditation. This is important also with Scriptural passages. It is better to let the person pray over the Scriptural passages, rather than over the director's interpretation of them.

The invitation is more than to «follow me.» Christ says to

«labor with me,» «suffer with me.» Not just to be with me but to «labor with me.» Now, that is quite a different thing. And «to suffer with me» is different again. Thus, at the same time that there is an appeal to one's generosity, there is an appeal directed to the person of Christ. Because they are a test of one's intention, the laboring and suffering bring reality to personal love.

One of the few places where Ignatius uses the word «love» before the «Contemplation to Attain Love of God» is found in the third point on the «Eternal King.» He speaks of «Those who wish to give greater proof of their love, and to distinguish themselves in whatever concerns the service of the eternal King and the Lord of all.» [97] Clearly, «Those who wish to give greater proof of their love, and to distinguish themselves» are those who are willing to be inconvenienced.

At the end of the meditation he suggests a more difficult offering of self: «I protest that it is my earnest desire and my deliberate choice, provided only it is for Thy greater service and praise, to imitate Thee in bearing all wrongs and all abuse and all poverty, both actual and spiritual, should Thy most holy majesty deign to choose and admit me to such a state and way of life.» [98] It reminds one of the prayers of Teilhard de Chardin and of the great acts of consecration religious used to make in the novitiate.

At this point the retreatant is merely hoping he is capable of making this kind of offering. The prayer expresses the way he feels at the moment; it is the way he would like it to be. The offering itself will become more detailed and more explicit as he moves through the Exercises. The present exercise on Christ the King is a sort of second «Principle and Foundation» for the rest of the retreat, and the offering at the end is similar to the «Third Kind of Humility» and the prayer in the «Contemplation to Attain Love of God.» But even now he begins to make it his

120

own. This prayer suggests the difference between an active and a passive acceptance of suffering. It is a great grace for a man to be able to accept passively the crosses that are given to him. One should truly pray for that grace. But the attitude expressed in this prayer goes beyond that. It involves not merely accepting the crosses that are imposed, but reaching for the cross with Christ. It embodies a positive desire to be with Christ as he reaches for his cross. Christ does so out of love for mankind. He does not reach for the cross in order to suffer, but in order to expre , his love.

At times a retreatant may become conscious of something more than a passive experience of God's love operating in him. An example of such passivity would be in the forgiveness of his sin. Sooner or later he begins to realize that the Exercises and the broader Christian spirituality demand more active expressions of love. Man is somehow responsible for the universe. God has created him as a free being. In that freedom he may reject God's love, but he may also respond to it actively. And while man's response to God's love is totally God's operation, it is also totally man's. Right here in the «Kingdom of Christ» he is presented with the responsibility of becoming a generous instrument for the redemption of the world.

There is a maxim of Ignatius that you may have heard, perhaps in a garbled version. The more traditional reading of the maxim is, «Trust in God as though the entire success of affairs depended on you and nothing on God. Accept totally your responsibility, but apply yourself to your work as though God were to accomplish everything and you nothing.» [6] Now, this is rather different from what you may have heard. Typically many versions start out to clarify the paradox of this traditional version and end up giving it an opposite meaning, such as this one: «Trust in God as though he were to accomplish everything and you nothing; but apply yourself to your work as though the entire success of affairs depended on you and nothing on God.» But this formulation destroys the paradox in the maxim and tends to make it pelagian.

As the Christian goes to labor with Christ, then, he prays to God as though the whole work was his own to accomplish. He prays for enlightenment, for discernment, for strength, for all the human qualities that are needed in order to achieve the thing humanly. He is responsible for the effort. But he trusts in God so highly that he is at peace in his work, knowing that the success of the venture is God's, not man's. This may help me to appreciate what must be my response to the call of Christ the King.

I have noted that the offering at the end is a very difficult one and may only express what the retreatant would hope to do. It is important to remember also that this meditation is transitional. It is meant to bring the person to the awareness that he can do something for the Lord. He feels he is more than a person who is receiving Christ's grace passively in the forgiveness of sins, but receives it actively as well by loving and following Christ. This meditation takes on more meaning as the retreatant works his way through the life of Christ and the key exercises of the «Second Week.» It is also true that as he proceeds he will become more conscious of sin, of his lack of gratitude and of his dependence on God.

Ignatius was a great judge of character, I think. He felt that, if grounds for magnanimity of soul did not appear in the «First Week,» then there was no point in presenting the person with the meditation on the «Kingdom» and moving him through the other «Three Weeks.» In such a case he would only give the exercises of the «First Week,» emphasizing an awareness that God loved the person and had forgiven his sin. He would also give him the method of examination of conscience and other prayers. [18]

It is not as if Christ is not present in the «First Week.» He is certainly present there as savior, especially in the colloquy of the «First Exercise,» where he is hanging on the cross. But the «Kingdom» meditation demands a magnanimity and a generosity of soul that may not be found in everybody. And that is where discernment is needed. If you cannot decide clearly, then I would suggest that you give the «Call of the King» and some other prayer periods on the life of Christ until you become more certain. Only after this should you give the «Two Standards,» «Three Classes of Men,» «Three Kinds of Humility,» and similar exercises.

CHAPTER 8

DISCERNMENT — FIRST WEEK

*Let me put it like this: if you are guided by the Spirit
you will be in no danger of yielding to self-indulgence,
since self-indulgence is the opposite of the Spirit, the
Spirit is totally against such a thing, and it is precisely
because the two are so opposed that you do not always
carry out your good intentions. If you are led by the
Spirit, no law can touch you. When self-indulgence is
at work, the results are obvious: fornication, gross in-
decency and sexual irresponsibility; idolatry and sorcery;
feuds and wrangling, jealousy, bad temper and quarrels;
disagreements, factions, envy; drunkenness, orgies and
similar things. I warn you now, as I warned you before:
those who behave like this will not inherit the kingdom
of God. What the Spirit brings is very different: love,
joy, peace, patience, kindness, goodness, trustfulness,
gentleness and self-control. There can be no law against
things like that, of course. You cannot belong to Christ
Jesus unless you crucify all self-indulgent passions and
desires.*

*Since the Spirit is our life, let us be directed by the
Spirit. We must stop being conceited, provocative and
envious. (Ga 5:16-26)*

Since Vatican II, the subject of discernment has
come to the fore. It appears very often in the documents of the

124

Council, which emphasized the fact that not merely bishops and religious superiors but any Christian can be inspired by the Spirit. The Council also gave a new recognition to man's free will. Moreover, in recent years a new phenomenon called Pentecostalism has arisen among Catholics. This has given added impetus to research and reflection on the movement of spirits.

Let me first mention some helpful works on the topic. In paperback there is an English translation of an article from *Dictionnaire de Spiritualité* — actually a series of articles by different scholars — under the title *Discernment of Spirits.* [7] It presents the historical development of the discernment of spirits and discusses the contribution of the Ignatian rules. [313-336] There have been a number of very good articles on discernment of spirits in *The Way*.[8] The article in *Sacramentum Mundi*[9] is valuable. The volume entitled *Finding God in All Things,* which is a translation of articles from the French periodical *Christus,* contains two good articles on this subject. Possibly the most penetrating theological study is an article by Karl Rahner, «Individual Knowledge in Ignatius Loyola,» which is included in his book, *The Dynamic Element in the Church.*[10]

Ignatius headlines his treatment of discernment as follows: «*Rules for understanding to some extent the different movements produced in the soul and for recognizing those that are good to admit them, and those that are bad, to reject them. These rules are more suited to the first week.*» [313] In these rules it is possible and necessary to prescind from whether good and evil spirits exist as such. The very question itself can interfere with effective discernment of good and evil tendencies.

What is necessary is to accept the fact that there is an evil force at work in our universe which is independent of ourselves. Likewise, we have to accept the existence of a good force that is outside us and independent of us. (This says nothing about the

125

origin of these forces such as the dualistic philosophy of Manicheanism proposes.) Good and evil operate within us as well.

When we speak about «evil spirits,» we are talking about these forces of evil that are independent of us. Where they come from is not always significant. What is important is to understand the movement of spirits that occurs in ourselves or in others. At times it may be necessary to distinguish whether these movements are psychological or spiritual, whether they originate in the person or outside the person.

What I am trying to say is that if you wish to define the devil as the sum total of personal evil in the universe or as an individual personal being, either definition is consistent with the Ignatian rules of discernment. The important thing is that, granted such forces are operating on us, we can make judgments on them and discern their nature. The words, «evil spirits» and «good spirits,» or «bad angel» and «good angel,» should not become a «hang-up,» a cause of distraction from the essential task of discovering where the real forces of good and evil (to which such terms refer) are in fact leading us.

In considering the «Rules for Discernment» suited to the «First Week,» it may be useful to cite the full text of Ignatius here and to introduce comments from time to time where clarifications seem warranted.

> *Rule 1:* In the case of those who go from one mortal sin to another, the enemy is ordinarily accustomed to propose apparent pleasures. He fills their imagination with sensual delights and gratifications, the more readily to keep them in their vices and increase the number of their sins.
>
> With such persons the good spirit uses a method which is the reverse of the above. Making use of the

126

light of reason, he will rouse the sting of conscience and fill them with remorse. [314]

The enemy here is the enemy of all mankind. He is also my personal enemy. Even if the movements that I am experiencing arise from the concupiscence of my own flesh, he will try to make use of them to destroy me.

> *Rule 2:* In the case of those who go on earnestly striving to cleanse their souls from sin and who seek to rise in the service of God our Lord to greater perfection, the method pursued is the opposite of that mentioned in the first rule.
>
> Then it is characteristic of the evil spirit to harass with anxiety, to afflict with sadness, to raise obstacles backed by fallacious reasonings that disturb the soul. Thus he seeks to prevent the soul from advancing.
>
> It is characteristic of the good spirit, however, to give courage and strength, consolations, tears, inspirations, and peace. This He does by making all easy, by removing all obstacles so that the soul goes forward in doing good. [315]

The experience varies with each person's moral behavior. If an individual is going from bad to worse, then in a sense he is the home of the evil spirit. Such a person is so sensual and so self-centered that the whole movement of his being tends to encourage and participate in the disordered acts listed by Paul in Galatians 5. His life is sensual to the extent that he cannot understand anyone who is not sensual or self-centered. The evil spirits are at home in a person dominated by thoughts of sensuality or pride or jealousy or envy. They enter and leave with ease. But the good spirit in that case is a disturbing influence. His entry makes a lot of noise. He stings the conscience of the sensual man.

On the other hand, the person going from good to better is the home of the good spirit. For people of that kind the good spirit enters gently and quietly. It encourages them with strength and hope. It is the evil spirit that causes anxiety and disturbance, tribulation and sadness.

It follows that in directing another you should find out whether or not the evil spirit feels at home with him. Perhaps his first need is to confess his sins. If his condition is habitually sinful, but you assume you are dealing with someone who is advancing in the spiritual life, then you could easily misjudge the movements occurring in his heart.

To speak in the older terminology, it is important to know whether he is in the «state of grace.» And if so, does he really desire to progress in the Lord? Is he constantly giving in to himself? You might think that any individual making a retreat would belong to the more advanced group. But sometimes this is not the case. It depends on the reasons or pressures that have prevailed on him to come on retreat.

> *Rule 3:* I call it consolation when an interior movement
> is aroused in the soul, by which it is inflamed with love
> of its Creator and Lord, and as a consequence, can love
> no creature on the face of the earth for its own sake, but
> only in the Creator of them all. [316]

This definition makes it clear that consolation is not merely gratification or pleasure. While it may be related to other persons or objects, it must include the persons of the Trinity. For example, an interior movement may arise from the love one has for another human person, and this kind of emotional experience may resemble spiritual consolation. But it can be the beginning of spiritual consolation only when that human love is directly related to the love of God.

128

> It is likewise consolation when one sheds tears that move to the love of God, whether it be because of sorrow for sins, or because of the sufferings of Christ our Lord, or for any other reason that is immediately directed to the praise and service of God. [316]

When they accompany sorrow or true joy, or when they flow from compassionate union with the sufferings of Christ, tears are an expression of consolation. One way or another a person who is deeply consoled by God needs to give vent to his feelings. At times his relationship to Christ may release him from the narrow bonds of egotism, take him out of himself and overflow in tears. I should add, of course, that all tears do not come from consolation but only the «tears that move to the love of God.»

> Finally, I call consolation every increase of faith, hope, and love, and all interior joy that invites and attracts to what is heavenly and to the salvation of one's soul by filling it with peace and quiet in its Creator and Lord. [316]

Now, many people think that only the first sentence of this rule where a certain sensible or emotional activity is mentioned, truly describes consolation. But here Ignatius points out that every increase of faith, hope, and love is consolation. Often one who is praying becomes downcast because he does not feel that the Lord is giving him any consolation. And, of course, he begins to suspect that by doing something wrong he has failed to earn the consolation: «Perhaps the Lord does not love me.» But when you question him, you find that his faith or hope or love has been increased. He has discovered a new meaning to life. And yet he does not think that he has been consoled — simply because he did not have tears or some other intense experience that might be described as an «interior movement by which the soul is inflamed with love of its Creator and Lord.» His notion of consolation is incomplete.

> *Rule 4:* I call desolation what is entirely the opposite of what is described in the third rule, as darkness of soul, turmoil of spirit, inclination to what is low and earthly, restlessness rising from many disturbances and temptations which lead to want of faith, want of hope, want of love. The soul is wholly slothful, tepid, sad and separated, as it were, from its Creator and Lord. For just as consolation is the opposite of desolation, so the thoughts that spring from consolation are the opposite of those that spring from desolation. [317]

These experiences of desolation would seem to apply to the person who is going from good to better in the «First Week.» When there is this darkness of soul, turmoil of spirit, inclination to what is low and earthly, tepidity, and sadness, then some questions may help to discover what its occasion or cause may be. True, to discover the source does not mean to take it away. But the person will at least begin to understand himself and to see how he is moved by different spirits.

«Low and earthly» probably means «sensual,» — troubled with sexual temptations. It is a very trying experience to be constantly pursued by that kind of temptation. And, as a person experiences depression and desolation, then hope and love decrease. He becomes fainthearted in the service of the Lord. He loses all generosity, all magnanimity of soul.

Of course, when the person gives into these temptations and abandons himself to self-centered sexual experience, this is not desolation. Such a person is among those going from bad to worse. [314] This applies also to the phantasy world of ambition,

130

power, anger, hatred, bitterness, and so on: everything depends on whether one is fighting or enjoying these tendencies.

> *Rule 5:* In time of desolation we should never make any change, but remain firm and constant in the resolution and decision which guided us the day before the desolation, or in the decision to which we adhered in the preceding consolation. For just as in consolation the good spirit guides and counsels us, so in desolation the evil spirit guides and counsels. Following his counsels we can never find the way to a right decision. [318]

The time of desolation is precisely when people are strongly impelled to make a change. But it is the worst time to change since it is itself an occasion for the evil spirit to act. When you are directing someone and he wishes to make an important change during desolation, you should help him to put it off until he is in consolation. Sometimes this will take a long time, but it is essential to be patient. When we are going from good to better, the good spirit is strengthening us and the evil spirit is tempting us to change. In the time of desolation, then, we can never make the right decision.

> *Rule 6:* Though in desolation we must never change our former resolutions, it will be very advantageous to intensify our activity against the desolation. We can insist more upon prayer, upon meditation, and on much examination of ourselves. We can make an effort in a suitable way to do some penance. [319]

It is truly remarkable what penance can achieve when one is in desolation. Often it can knock a person out of his desolate condition by giving a sort of jolt to his sullen spirit.

Rule 7: When one is in desolation, he should be mindful that God has left him to his natural powers to resist the different agitations and temptations of the enemy in order to try him. He can resist with the help of God, which always remains, though he may not clearly perceive it. For though God has taken from him the abundance of fervor and overflowing love and the intensity of His favors, nevertheless, he has sufficient grace for eternal salvation. [320]

Rule 8: When one is in desolation, he should strive to persevere in patience. This reacts against the vexations that have overtaken him. Let him consider, too, that consolation will soon return. ... [321]

These directives are easy to understand and approve — in the time of consolation. But in the time of desolation we usually fail to appreciate them. Unfortunately, patience is the last thing a desolate man can lay his hands on.

The last sentence is more encouraging. It is my experience with people long acquainted with the spiritual life that they are conscious that ups and downs, moments of consolation and desolation, are inevitable. They understand this rule. But beginners find it difficult to believe. They are tempted very strongly to give up. All sorts of persuasion are needed to keep them praying, lest they change in a time of desolation.

Rule 9: The principal reasons why we suffer from desolation are three: The first is because we have been tepid and slothful or negligent in our exercises of piety, and so through our own fault spiritual consolation has been taken away from us. [322]

The regular examination of conscience and review of prayer

can help detect this cause of desolation. If an individual has been careless about recollection or unfaithful to his spiritual exercises, it is quite obvious where the trouble lies. But how does this fit in with lack of grace? The second and third reasons given by Ignatius may answer that question.

> The second reason is because God wishes to try us, to see how much we are worth, and how much we will advance in His service and praise when left without the generous reward of consolations and signal favors. [322]

Desolation forces me to question the selflessness of my love. Do I love God merely because I enjoy those interior movements that inflame my heart with love? Or can I persevere in loving him, keep on doing the job, even in desolation, even without those singular graces that Ignatius speaks about?

> The third reason [and this is the one that applies to most of us] is because God wishes to give us a true knowledge and understanding of ourselves, so that we may have an intimate perception of the fact that it is not within our power to acquire and attain great devotion, intense love, tears, or any other spiritual consolation; but that all this is the gift and grace of God our Lord. God does not wish us to build on the property of another, to rise up in spirit in a certain pride and vainglory and attribute to ourselves the devotion and other effects of spiritual consolation. [322]

A thirty-day retreat should give you enough experience to appreciate the truth of what Ignatius is saying. But let me use the example of a walk in the warm sunlight. The birds are singing, you are praying about creation, and God is almost tangible to you. But on another day you take the same walk with the same sun shining and the same birds singing, but you experience no awareness of God at all.

The thirty-day retreat provides time enough to realize that consolation does not result from anything we have done. It is strictly a grace from God. Thus, the Lord may allow me to be desolate at times in order to impress upon me the fact of my pelagianism, my desire to control God. He wants me to abandon the mistaken notion that I can command consolation to come and desolation to go by an act of the will.

In this rule Ignatius covers the reasons for desolation when a person is going from good to better. He can be in desolation through his own fault, or the Lord may allow desolation in order to try him or so that he may gain the intimate knowledge that consolation is strictly his gift. When we come to discuss the rules of the «Second Week,» we will discover that there are two basic kinds of consolation: the consolation which expresses God's love through some intervening experience and the consolation that results from the Lord's own immediate presence. But in the «First Week» rules Ignatius is speaking more about those consolations from God which are indirect expressions of his love.

> *Rule 10:* When one enjoys consolation, let him consider how he will conduct himself during the time of the ensuing desolation, and store up a supply of strength as defense against that day. [323]

> *Rule 11:* He who enjoys consolation should take care to humble himself and lower himself as much as possible. Let him recall how little he is able to do in time of desolation, when he is left without such grace of consolation.
>
> On the other hand, one who suffers desolation should remember that by making use of the sufficient

grace offered him, he can do much to withstand all his enemies. Let him find his strength in his Creator and Lord. [324]

Not only is Ignatius aware of the oscillations in a person's life, whether intellectual, emotional or spiritual, but he knows how to deal with them. How dull life would be if things never changed! Some people are sanguine in temperament, and this effects their spiritual life. Their highs are so high and their lows are so low that life for them is like a ride on a roller coaster. If they can recognize this range of emotion, then your direction may help them level off into a curve like that of the trigonometric sine curve. This may be done by some simple expression such as «prepare your soul for desolation» when you see them too highly consoled. Similarly, when they are too far down, try to lift them up with reminders of God's mercy and with other considerations. [cf. 7] You should teach them this procedure; it is important for them to learn how to handle their own problems.

Ignatius's directive «He who enjoys consolation should take care to humble himself,» needs expansion. When the person is in a state of high consolation, his tendency is to take possession of it as his own and to attribute it to himself. This is an occasion for spiritual pride, for grasping as one's due the gifts which the Lord has freely given. In the time of consolation then, he ought to pray constantly for humility. He should adopt the attitude our Lady expresses so eloquently in her *Magnificat*. As Ignatius says, it is a time to humble oneself, to recall how useless one is in the time of desolation, how little strength one has then.

At the end of these Rules [325-327] Ignatius describes the devil and gives him his true title, «the enemy of mankind.» He compares him to a quarrelsome woman, to a false lover, and to an army general. Possibly you have experienced his activity in

135

these different ways. Often the face the devil shows to you depends on your spiritual state at the time of temptation. If you are in consolation and things are going well, then it is easy to see the devil with the characteristics of a vixen and to treat him as a strong man might a troublesome woman. But when the devil is not so easily recognized, the tendency is to become discouraged and to back away in fear into one's own self-centeredness. But, knowing our enemy's true nature, Ignatius advises in every case to face him with strength. Spiritual writers often describe the evil spirit as a chained dog. The dog makes a frightening noise with his barking, snarling and growling, but as long as you stay beyond that chain, he cannot hurt you.

The second description of the devil is probably the most important. Our enemy is compared to a false lover who desires to keep everything hidden and secret. When you are giving spiritual direction and you feel the counselee is not as open as he might be, sometimes it helps if you give him the rules for discernment. When he reads these rules, he may discover that his experience is as old as Ignatius and older, since «the devil was a liar from the beginning.» He may then be encouraged to speak to you about his hidden fears and anxieties.

It is my own personal experience and the experience of people I have directed that often when one is agitated and disturbed, the mere act of going to the spiritual counselor brings the light and peace one needs. The mere willingness to be open with someone may take away the anxiety.

Sometimes, soon after a person has come in, he says: «Oh, I came in with such a heavy burden, Father, but it is all gone.» Still it is good to ask what it is, so that he can get it out in the open. For secrecy is a powerful weapon in the devil's arsenal. He seeks above all to remain hidden. He hates to be discovered:

In the same way, when the enemy of our human nature tempts a just soul with his wiles and seductions, he earnestly desires that they be received secretly and kept secret. But if one manifests them to a confessor, or to some other spiritual person who understands his deceits and malicious designs, the evil one is very much vexed. For he knows that he cannot succeed in his evil undertaking, once his evident deceits have been revealed. [326]

In his third way of attacking a man, the devil resembles an army general. He explores a man's fortification, discovers the strong points and the weak points, and only then makes his attack. One of the purposes of the «First Week» of the Exercises is for the retreatant to discover his own strong and weak points so that he will be conscious of where the devil will attack. It is important to know our strengths as well as our weaknesses; maybe the truest source of strength is our ability to cry, «Lord, have mercy.»

One principle mentioned in our discussion of the «Kingdom» meditation will be crucial in all spiritual direction. It is that the director must be patient and open to the particular impact of an exercise or Scriptural passage the retreatant is praying over. The tendency of a director is to allow no opportunity for the Holy Spirit to impart his consolation. Instead the director may wish to give his own consolation to the one who is making the Exercises. And that can have little value.

As you may have gathered from our discussion of the «First Week» and of the «Kingdom,» since those exercises touch a man at the deepest part of his being, he can expect a movement of spirits to occur. He will react favorably or unfavorably. He will find them consoling or difficult. The movement of spirits is known precisely by his individual reaction to the exercise or the Scripture that is given to him.

If you supply the passage on the prodigal son, for example, one person will react to it differently than another. There is an advantage in knowing the Scriptural passage, for then it is easier to appreciate what is happening to the exercitant. It also helps you to determine the material of the next prayer period in your dialogue with the exercitant.

Of course, great freedom must be maintained here. It is important that you give the retreatant something to pray over, either one of the exercises, or the *Imitation of Christ,* or *The Life of Christ,* or the life of a saint, but preferably a Scriptural passage. In some instances very challenging texts from Scripture occasion a significant reaction. Does the retreatant find consolation or desolation? Is there great fear and turmoil? Or is there a growth of faith, hope, and love?

Outside the context of the Exercises, it may be asked, how can a director know which way to proceed, or what Scripture passages to give? Usually, after talking for some time to an individual, you will discover his state of soul. He has lost hope, or faith, or has no desire to love. If he is in consolation, then it is easy to give direction. Tell him to continue in the same way and to prepare himself for desolation.

But one of the difficulties in spiritual counseling comes from the fact that people often seek counsel only when they are down. You should first try to find the particular area of desolation. Your counselee may be experiencing loneliness, for example, or sexual temptation, or a sense of failure. For each of these cases it is good to have certain Scriptural passages for him to pray over. Often all that is needed is for him to hear you say, «That's right, that's reality,» or «We're all sinners, we all experience our weakness,» or «Who do you think you are anyway, Jesus Christ?»

In short, he may need to be reminded that he is a human being and that life is tough for everyone. Then it will make sense to suggest he pray on the Agony in the Garden. Possibly he will see that life is not as difficult as the Agony in the Garden, and he may experience an uplift of soul. Perhaps he will take as his own St. Paul's consoling text, «The weak things of the world God has chosen to confound the strong,» and say to himself, «Thank God, I'm one of those weak things.»

But sometimes his desolation may come from not accepting his sinfulness. He does not want to face the fact that he is a sinner and is trying to escape the full reality of his condition. Then a text like the parable of the pharisee and the publican may help him. Whatever the special need, progress takes time. One of the beauties about a thirty-day retreat is that you do get to know the retreatant and some of the movements of spirits that occur in him. If you continue in a counseling situation afterwards, you will be able to help him even more.

To discern how a person is responding to God's grace or what his vocation is often takes more than thirty days. It is an on-going process. Most congregations have at least one year of novitiate, if not two, in addition to the long period before final vows or ordination. These long periods are needed to discern a vocation.

All this talk of consolation and desolation may seem unreal. The person may only be having an off day, and one of the first things to be discerned, of course, is whether or not his current experience is exceptional. It may have something to do with a passing biological condition: perhaps he had only three hours sleep the night before, perhaps he has been suffering from a toothache. There are many possible explanations for the feelings that come over a person.

Even so, after you have become familiar with the usual

range of your client's moods and with the particular physical and psychic trends in his life, you will find at times that the best conditions for a healthy reaction are disturbed by desolation. None of the expected biological or other factors are present. Experience will help you to identify changes that suggest a spiritual cause. The client himself can come to learn how to distinguish which movements within him occur on this higher level of awareness.

Not all consolations are peak experiences of an intimate love relationship with God. Sometimes there is only a peacefully calm sense that the Lord is present. In Galatians Paul lists a number of signs, such as patience, kindness, tenderness; these signify consolation and the ability to love. When you are discerning whether the good or evil spirit is at work, remember that it is «by their fruits you shall know them.» But the words «consolation» and «desolation» are very technical terms as Ignatius defines them. I seldom use this vocabulary when I am giving a retreat. Instead I speak of comfort, of peace and quiet, of calmness, and of union with God — all the words Ignatius uses in defining consolation.

Scripture passages and the Exercises can easily be used together. But many directors use Scripture alone in shorter retreats; they never use the Exercises themselves. In a shorter retreat Scripture can produce the same results without the hangups that retreatants sometime experience in the Ignatian Exercises. All the same, I think it is true that certain exercises of Ignatius make a person consider the basic relationships with Christ much more forcibly than most Scripture texts can achieve. Of course, there were times when Christ himself was very forceful, as the following words indicate: «Unless a man hate father, mother, brother, and sister, he cannot be my disciple.» Or think of his rebuke to Peter, «Get behind me, Satan.» But even these words are not as pointed and concentrated as some of the exercises are.

Use the instrument that you are at ease with. The only precaution I would make is that you know the ascetical principles involved and that you be clear about what you are hoping to effect through the Scripture passages that you give. Once it is assigned, be relaxed with the Scriptural text you are using. You give it with the purpose that the passage will occasion growth in faith, or hope, or love, or some other virtue. That is as far as you can go.

You do not know whether the particular text will in fact produce the results you desire. That is the function of the Spirit. He may have other — and better — designs for your client. In any case, you will have provided material that centers on the problem as best you have been able to discern it, and after the Spirit has brought about some new development, whatever it may be, you can then turn your attention to what has actually happened and move ahead from there.

CHAPTER 9

CONTEMPLATION — THE HIDDEN LIFE

If our life in Christ means anything to you, if love can persuade at all, or the Spirit that we have in common, or any tenderness and sympathy, then be united in your convictions and united in your love, with a common purpose and a common mind. That is the one thing which would make me completely happy. There must be no competition among you, no conceit; but everybody is to be self-effacing. Always consider the other person to be better than yourself, so that nobody thinks of his own interests first but everybody thinks of other people's interests instead. In your minds you must be the same as Christ Jesus: His state was divine, yet he did not cling to his equality with God but emptied himself to assume the condition of a slave, and became as men are; and being as all men are, he was humbler yet, even to accepting death, death on a cross. But God raised him high and gave him the name which is above all other names so that all beings *in the heavens, on earth and in the underworld,* should bend the knee *at the name of Jesus and that every tongue should acclaim Jesus Christ as Lord, to the glory of God the Father. (Ph 2:1-11)*

The contemplation on the Incarnation follows at once upon the «Kingdom» meditation with its call to the exercitant, «to labor with me, that by following me in suffering, he may follow me in glory.» The retreatant has made an offering to the King, at least tentatively. Now he will go through the life of the King, his leader, seeking the grace of «deep-felt knowledge of our Lord made man for me, that I may the better love and follow him.»

And so he enters into the first labor of Christ, the Incarnation. The strategy of the Trinity in bringing about the redemption of the world begins with the Second Person becoming man. The composition of place is highly imaginative and anthropomorphic: the retreatant is directed to place himself with the Father, the Son, and the Holy Spirit, looking down on the great round surface of the world, in order to see what is happening on earth. He should strive to gain the Trinity's perspective of the universe and to enter into the cosmic dimension of reality.

If you go to Europe and visit its many museums and art galleries, you will discover that Christian art gives precedence to two phases in the life of Christ, the infancy and the passion. There are also great masterpieces on the public life of Christ and on his resurrection and ascension, but the infancy and passion are more frequent subjects of medieval and renaissance art. I do not know what this means unless it be that his infancy and passion tend to emphasize the humanity of Christ.

When we consider the first two contemplations, those on the Incarnation and the Nativity, we find that a dominant factor in both is poverty. The emptying out of God, the poverty of God, the humility of God is ever present. A couple of years ago, a young religious came to me to make a retreat. I asked him, «Where do you want to start?» he replied, «Well, I've been dealing with people a lot, and I am very interested in the human dimension and the way God enters the world through human beings.» Accordingly, we decided to begin with the exercise on the Incarnation. At the next interview, when I asked him about his prayer, he agreed that it went fairly well. There was only one thing in the exercise that really upset him. It was where Ignatius says that the divine Persons are looking «down upon the whole surface of the earth, and behold all nations in great blindness, going down to death and descending into hell.» [106] Since he was unable to accept this statement, we discussed it in detail. The upshot was that we realized he ought to begin further back — with the exercises on sin and hell. He had not been prepared to grasp the poverty of God in the face of sin, the merciful love that brought the divine Son into our fallen world to save all men.

After the exercise on the «Kingdom,» about three days are given to the infancy and the hidden life of Christ. These exercises are examples of Ignatian contemplation. Since there are different explanations of contemplation, this may be the place to dwell on the topic for a moment. Contemplation, strictly speaking, is the assumption of a person into the presence of God, or into one or other of the mysteries of Christ. But at this point Ignatius is not dealing with contemplation in that strict sense but merely presenting a method of prayer.

Any method of prayer is valuable mainly at the beginning of a prayer period. When the period of prayer is going well, different ways of praying may be given to the person as he proceeds: God moves him in this or that direction. So, you may start with any one of these methods — meditation, contemplation, application of the senses, vocal prayer, first method of prayer, second method of prayer, third method of prayer, reading of Scripture — then shift to another. Once prayer starts, the Lord is supposed to take over. If he does not do so, then you should keep on using the method you began with.

Meditation tends to be discursive, that is, in meditating a

man thinks over some truth or virtue. Contemplation, on the other hand, seeks a deep-felt response by being present to a person or event rather than by thinking about him or about his teachings and virtues. The act of presence is basic to contemplation. It is an attempt to be present with Christ in a given mystery.

Ignatius has the retreatant spend two or three days on the hidden life, using this method of prayer. This prepares him for the contemplations of the public life that come after the «Two Standards» and the «Three Classes of Men,» in which the person has been seeking the will of God in the presence of Christ.

This «contemplative» experience of prayer is especially well adapted for discernment of spirits, when a person is trying to find out what the Lord wants. It is a very relaxed form of prayer. It is also very simple. The retreatant has merely to be «there» in the mystery; he is to place himself at the scene and then to let the Spirit take over. This approach to prayer requires less mental effort and sets one free, like a bird gliding in the wind. In such an atmosphere the Spirit can move in and out of the person's mind and heart much more easily than in a meditative form of prayer. The individual himself and his director are able to note the movement of spirits, the consolations and desolations that affect him concerning a decision, while he is present at the different mysteries of Christ's public life.

During the Exercises a director often insists that the review take place only after the prayer is completed. The tendency may be to worry how the prayer is going during the exercise itself. But in contemplation you should place yourself in the mystery and simply let it go. Sometimes you will look at the time and find that only three minutes have gone by. But at other times more than an hour has passed. You are aware that you have not fallen asleep, but something has taken place and you know it.

This «something» should be considered in the review of

prayer. There may be one aspect of the mystery that has made a deep impression on you. Ignatius advises you to keep returning to that point in repetitions until you feel satisfied that the Spirit has led you as far into it as you need. There is no necessity to take up further mysteries as long as the Lord is drawing you more deeply into union with himself through the mystery you are presently contemplating. As Jesus said about Martha's sister Mary, the contemplative sitting at his feet, «One thing is necessary.»

Contemplation allows freedom for the Spirit to operate. Sometimes vocal prayer, or discursive prayer, or meditative prayer may lead to the same relaxed attitude before God. This freedom is one reason why the exercitant is given two or three days to practice contemplation. Ignatius then presents the «Two Standards,» which is a meditation. After that the exercitant resumes the contemplations on the public life of Christ so that the Spirit may operate freely once more.

Thus, he is to open his whole being to the mystery that he is contemplating. Since God acts within every person in order to bring his divine life and love into fruition, the retreatant tries in this kind of prayer to dispose himself for the Lord's operations. Prayer does not consist in becoming empty of self-centeredness, but in being filled with the presence of God. The negative emptying out of self is necessary. But it is only a preliminary to being filled with the presence of God. It is an approach to the Person who is in and above all persons.

Even when asking things of God in Christ, the petition is an opening of self, a gift of self to God. One has to expose himself, sometimes active in prayer, sometimes passive. St. Teresa speaks of grace coming like water, sometimes as from a well, sometimes as from a spring, sometimes as from a tap, and sometimes as from the sky in the form of rain. Sometimes you have to pull up the pail; sometimes you simply turn the tap; and sometimes it just comes by itself.

This contemplative method of prayer can be understood easily enough by noting the power of memory and imagination in ordinary life. It is not difficult for most people at one time or another to fall into a reverie. They become oblivious to what surrounds them and are caught up in the scene or circumstances of former events that made a deep impression on them. They hear what is said, see the actions, gestures and expressions of those involved, and experience anew the mysterious meaning of what happened. It matters very little how long ago it was or where it took place — in New York, Vancouver, or Paris. One's whole self is preoccupied with that arresting moment. That is what memory and imagination can do.

In Ignatian contemplation you form the habit of losing yourself, through the same powers, in sacred events of great significance. After some initial practice, you can learn how to stay with the scene and its actions, to relax in the presence of those who speak and move, and to open yourself without reserve to what occurs so that you may receive a deep impression of its mysterious meaning.

Of course, there are different ways of being present to a mystery. Some people can only stand awkwardly at the door and observe as if from a distance. When reading a powerful novel, they are scarcely moved. They seem to stand aloof at a film or a drama. Others can more easily get lost in the action.

The ability to enter personally into a novel, or a movie, or a stage production is what Ignatius wants us to exercise in contemplating the mysteries of Christ's life. If a particular retreatant is unable to do it, at least to some degree, then the director should introduce him to another method of prayer. God will make his presence known in a manner suited to that individual.

The grace to be sought in these contemplations is a deep-felt knowledge of our Lord made man «for me.» [104] This is a special kind of knowledge. Consider, for example, the difference between conceptual and experiential ways of knowing. Knowledge is merely conceptual when learned through books, by thinking things out, or by hearing rational explanations. Of course, the knowledge sought in contemplation is not like that at all. Rather, it is gained through many personal contacts, by working side by side with another, by struggling with problems together, through intimate conversations and heart-to-heart exchanges. It is experiential, and it touches, not merely the top of the brain, but the whole self.

This experiential knowledge of our Lord, which can be gained in prayer, is also knowledge «through becoming.» We are «becoming» during the time of prayer since we are growing and relating to other persons in the presence of Jesus in these mysteries. Exactly how and why we can actually enter the mystery of Christ's life is a fascinating theological question. Here I can only refer to two good articles on the subject, one by Father David Stanley, S.J., in *Theological Studies* [11] and one by Father Joseph Whelan, S.J., in *The Way* [12].

The presence of Christ to the one contemplating can be considered from two viewpoints. It contains some of the aspects of Christ's presence in us through the indwelling of the Holy Spirit given to us at baptism. It also includes some aspects of his presence in the Eucharist. These two sacraments, then, can help us to understand somewhat how Christ may become present to the one contemplating the mysteries of his infancy and public life.

Through our baptism the Holy Spirit dwells in us as in a temple. Now, this Spirit is sent to us not only by the Father but also by Jesus himself: «the Holy Spirit, whom the Father will send in my name, will teach you everything and remind you of all I have said to you.» (Jn 14:26) «When the Advocate comes, whom I shall send to you from the Father ... he will be my witness.» (Jn 15:26) «He will glorify me, since all he tells you will be taken from what is mine.» (Jn 16:14)

The Spirit in our hearts through baptism is the Spirit of Jesus. We might say that the Spirit recalls to us everything that Jesus Christ taught to his apostles: in this sense his Spirit enlivens in us the «experiential memory» I spoke about above. In a mystical way, therefore, I am able to recall and be present at the mysteries of Christ's life. What is special about this method of presence is that it tends to be a return through history to the events of Christ's hidden and public life in Israel 2,000 years ago.

In the Eucharist, on the other hand, under the appearances of bread and wine Christ makes himself really present to us. The risen Lord, because he is beyond time enters into our time at this Eucharistic moment. Christ's presence before you in prayer is of the same order, and it depends in a similar way on the resurrection of Christ. In his resurrected state Christ is able to re-present the mysteries of his life just as he re-presents the Paschal Mystery in the Eucharist. There is a new dimension in the Eucharist that was not to be found at the Last Supper — the presence of the Christian! Obviously, you were not there at the first institution, but you can be present at the Eucharist today; that is an important difference. Christ has brought the Paschal Mystery before you in the Eucharist. Well, in a way analogous to your presence at the Eucharist, you can be present at the mysteries you contemplate. The Lord can do this because in his resurrected, glorified life he transcends time and space. He is the Lord of history and of the universe.

Thus, in this type of prayer, Ignatian contemplation, I begin with my memory recalling the events as depicted by Scripture, seeing the persons, hearing what they are saying and seeing what they are doing. But then with grace I become aware of the events in the mystery not in the sense that I imagine an historical event 2,000 years old but in the sense that Christ brings the mystery forward to me. Accordingly, in Ignatian contemplation there appear to be two movements; a going back in history through the Holy Spirit who recalls all things to me, but also and more important, Christ coming forward to me and presenting himself to me in the mystery I am contemplating. All of this, of course, is dependent on grace — the divine Persons' free presentation of themselves to me.

The reason for mentioning a theological explanation at this point is to insist that contemplative prayer is real; I am concerned lest the retreatant may feel it is only an exercise of the imagination. It is the Spirit that draws a man into the mystery. And he draws him into a real «mystical» presence and not merely into his imagination, just as a Christian comes into a real sacramental presence at the Eucharist. That is what contemplation means.

When a Christian is «at» the mystery, then he receives the gift of contemplation, strictly speaking. Ignatius suggests a method of opening oneself up to the mystery. But when one is actually «at» the mystery, that is due to a further action of God. Of course, every grace-full action comes from God, as St. Paul says: «It is God for his own loving purpose, who puts both the will and the action into you.» (Ph 2:13)

One can pray to Christ the infant, to Christ hanging on the cross, or to Christ forgiving the woman who washes his feet. This is possible because Christ takes up into his resurrected self all the events of his historical life. If I could put it this way, one is with the risen Christ in his infancy. He takes the believer

150

to his infancy and presents himself in his infancy. Or he presents himself on the cross. In this way the Christian is enabled by the Spirit to be present to the resurrected Christ, living and dying on the cross. He is talking to his followers from the cross. He communicates from the crib; he presents himself as a baby. And the believer stands in awe before the child. Mothers seem to be able to communicate with their babies. Most men stand in awe before an infant.

It is good to remember that this type of prayer has lasted through the Christian centuries. The faith of the Church has been operating in this way. My confidence in this type of prayer stems more from the fact that holy people in the Church have been doing it for two thousand years than from the fact that theologians can give me an explanation of it.

This prayer, then, goes beyond one's imagination. But it may only stay in the imagination. There is double movement here. The first is more or less the one that Ignatius indicates when he tells the exercitant to use his imagination to see the persons, to hear what they are saying and see what they are doing, and to draw some profit from this. That effort of the imagination with its accompanying reflection is good prayer in itself.

I am suggesting however, that it is merely the take-off point. The second movement occurs when you find that an hour has gone by unnoticed, and there has been some kind of experience of the Lord's presence. When you reflect over the prayer period, you are not aware that you picked up the baby and kissed him, or held him in your arms, or did any similar action. But there has come a new awareness of Christ in his mystery. This awareness is one of deep-felt knowledge.

In his study, *The Spiritual Exercises,*[4] Karl Rahner says that we do not lose the human Christ when he ascends to his Father because he takes up into himself everything of his earthly life.

151

Christ is that person who can hold every moment of his life in himself. Thus, when we go to the risen Christ in prayer, we can move into his «Nativity» by the power of His Spirit. All of this is a grace, of course — the resurrected Christ presenting himself in his mysteries and our receiving him because his Spirit is in us.

It is important for us to pray over the «Incarnation» and the other mysteries of Christ's life in order to gain deep-felt knowledge of Jesus. We understand more of what Christ means when he says, for instance, «Come and labor with me.» The relationship is such that any Christian can become another Christ, not only through baptism, which, of course, is essential, but even in his prayer life and his whole attitude.

In the contemplation on the «Incarnation» Ignatius suggests three scenes, the Trinity in heaven, the actions of mankind on the face of the earth, and the house in Nazareth. He narrows his focus dramatically like a skilled TV cameraman to convey the movement of God into human history through his tiny creature, Mary. The exercise closes with a colloquy: «I will think over what I ought to say to the Three Divine Persons, or to the eternal Word incarnate (not yet born, only a fertilized ovum), or to His Mother, our Lady.» [109] Thus, the grace to love and follow him is being refined. So, too, is the call of the King, «Come and labor with me.»

I would like to say at this point, regardless of the theological speculation about Christ's human knowledge, that the way Christians have been taught to pray on these mysteries did not interfere with the meaningful effect they have had in their lives. Today there is often a tendency to argue that if something does not fit modern theology, it is no good. We should be very wary of that kind of thinking. Two thousand years of faith and experience should make a difference. The theologians do not produce the faith; they try to explain it.

152

It may be true that the divinity of Christ was sometimes exaggerated in the spiritual life of Christians. For example, some writers assumed that in the garden of Gethsemane Christ knew every single one of his future followers and every single sin that men would commit. Now in the Word, in God the Son, this may be true, for in the Trinity all is in the «now.» But this kind of knowledge tends to neglect the human consciousness of Jesus. In Scripture we are told that «Jesus increased in wisdom, in stature, and in favour with God and men.» (Lk 2:52) There were areas of human ignorance in Christ, and his human knowledge has always raised serious theological questions.

We are aware that he knew everything in the divine «now.» Thus, Ignatius pictures the Trinity seeing everybody going to hell. There is a deep theological truth in this. If Jesus Christ had not become man, everyone would have gone to hell for he is the savior of the whole world. But that knowledge is in the Trinity. Once the Word becomes man, then there is another dimension of knowledge present. He has human as well as divine knowledge and consciousness.

In the spirituality of the past there was a tendency to fuse these two, and the fusion tended to reduce the role of the humanity of Christ. In a sense this destroyed the relevance of Jesus the man to the spiritual life of Christians. Some sort of theological explanation is needed. The basic point I am making is that, instead of going back in memory two thousand years into the mystery and being present to the historical Christ, Christ comes forward two thousand years and presents himself to me today in the mystery being contemplated. Moreover, in his human nature Jesus becomes present at a man's own mysteries of being. Such an explanation takes into account the human consciousness of Christ.

It is true that, when Jesus is in the «Agony in the Garden,»

153

he may have some type of human awareness that he is the savior of all men. But I suspect that Christ was very concerned about the failure of his mission with the Scribes and Pharisees and with the Jewish people as a whole. I also think that he was overwhelmed by knowledge of the physical pain he was going to suffer. So he kept repeating to the Father, «Take this cup away from me.» (Mk 14:36)

Now, the reason why I introduced this kind of explanation was to show that our contemplation is real and not just imaginary. When people in the Old Testament celebrated the passover meal, they felt that past events were made present to them. Similarly, at Mass it is not Calvary repeated over again but the paschal mystery being made present now so that Christians can participate in it. This is the precisely sacramental aspect of the mystery. In an analogous way, the word of Scripture is sacramental. It brings forward the mystery of Christ's life and makes it present.

The term «mystery» should be correctly understood. By «mystery» we do not mean a detective mystery, a problem, nor do we mean that it is false or fictional. What we mean is that there is a presence here that is beyond us and our understanding. We are launched into the mystery of divine presence, the continuing mystery of the presence of Christ. Contemplation implies our ability to enter into the presence of Christ, and his ability to enter into ours.

In contemplation then, we should realize that all we are doing is exposing ourselves to that presence. When the mystery becomes present, the Lord is operating in us — as he does analogously in the Eucharist. When we contemplate Jesus in the mysteries of his life, we are seeking to grasp something of Christ's experience as a man. But when we do this in a context of prayer and grace, then Christ makes us a part of his experience.

154

When a man is baptized, as we know from Romans 6, he is baptized into the death and resurrection of Christ. He becomes a part of Christ in this sense of «mystery.» He is united to him in such a way that the Spirit of Christ becomes his spirit. Newman has said somewhere that Christ is reborn in us and relives in us and dies again in us. Now, this is because my humanness, like Christ's, can be taken over by the Holy Spirit. Grace, in setting a man free, humanizes him to the full, makes him loved and graced as his being cries out to be loved and graced. He becomes, like Christ, the loved one of the Father and, in that creative love, must be fully human.

In contemplation, mystery becomes present so that man will know the Lord better. In order that he may the better love and follow his Lord, the one who contemplates wants Christ's human experience to somehow become his own. But it will be an ongoing experience: just as Christ continues to live in his mystical body, so Christ will continue to experience life in his individual members. Christ, we might say, is the primary model, his life is the model for every man's life. And this is real. Man is really present to Christ and, more important, Christ is really present to man.

In his historical experience Jesus was subject to limitations. He grew up in an historical setting, and he had human consciousness. But all of his experience was taken up into his risen body. When we speak about Christ's glorified state, we are really saying that Christ is present to the whole universe, not only to the Scribes and Pharisees, to Peter and to Mary Magdalene.

In the contemplation on the «Incarnation,» the Trinity is aware that, but for Christ, all men will go to hell. There are two different dimensions which Ignatius interweaves, the cosmic dimension and the human dimension. But in the second contemplation, that on the «Nativity,» the human dimension becomes dominant. The deep-felt knowledge of our Lord made man makes a greater impact there.

In the «Nativity» contemplation Ignatius advises the retreatant to place himself in the mystery as a little unworthy slave. This is not Scripture, but that is not the point. In this method of prayer you are to be there as an unworthy slave, a «little» unworthy slave.

For Ignatius, it is a significant factor. Because man was created to praise, reverence, and serve God, the exercitant is to present himself as a servant to Mary and Joseph and the child, and he is to show homage and reverence.

The third point must also be noted: the Lord will be «born in extreme poverty.» Here the strategy of the Trinity, of which we are to be aware is clearly revealed: «This will be to see and consider what they are doing, for example, making the journey and laboring that our Lord might be born in extreme poverty, and that after many labors, after hunger, thirst, heat, and cold, after insults and outrages, He might die on the cross, and all this for me.» [116]

Thus, the theme of the Kingdom appears again: «to labor with me, to suffer with me, that he might be glorified with me.» And it also points forward to the «Two Standards,» and the «Three Kinds of Humility.» It points back not only to the «Kingdom» but to the «Principle and Foundation» as well. The grace the retreatant seeks is to unite himself more closely with Christ's humanity; he wants deep-felt knowledge of our Lord made man for him. He asks for this deep-felt knowledge of our Lord, not insofar as he is God, but insofar as he is made man.

The fifth contemplation of the day is the «Application of the Senses.» It should be done at the end of the day, after the retreatant has contemplated four times; the soul is then full and able to apply the senses. This form of prayer is a method of

156

contemplating with one's whole being. As you read through the exercise, you notice that the first two points consist in seeing and hearing in the imagination the persons, contemplating and meditating on the details and circumstances in which they are placed, and then in drawing some fruit from what has been seen or heard. But the third point is «to smell the infinite fragrance, and to taste the infinite sweetness of the divinity.» [124] Well, Ignatius certainly moves quickly from the imagination to something more ethereal: «Likewise to apply these senses to the soul and its virtues, and to all according to the person we are contemplating, and to draw fruit from this.» [124] There is a movement beyond seeing and hearing the physical things and physical persons to contemplating things spiritual.

Hugo Rahner has a chapter on the «Application of the Senses» in *Ignatius the Theologian* [13]. He points out that Scripture occasionally suggests this sensuous way of approaching the reality of God. «Will your jealousy burn like fire?» Have you ever felt the burn of jealousy? «Your hand shall guide me and hold me fast.» «May he let his face shine upon us.» «Take refuge in the shelter of your wings.» «Taste and see the goodness of the Lord.» «Sweeter than syrup or honey from the cone.» «How sweet to my palate are your promises.» The above expressions are all taken from the Psalms, but the Song of Songs may be considered an extended «Application of the Senses.» In fact, «We are Christ's incense to God for those who are being saved,» St. Paul says. (2 Co 2:15)

Thus, the «Application of the Senses» moves into the spiritual senses. We experience this when we feel a desire to touch and to kiss a revered object. The totality of our being becomes involved in the mystery. Some people do it through a word such as «silence»: «When peaceful silence lay over all and night had run the half of her swift course, down from the heavens, from the royal throne, leapt your all powerful Word.» (Wis 18:14,15) The «Application of the Senses» is an attempt to move the mystery into the whole person. Words like jealousy, goodness, humility and joy may help as their more profound implications are savored.

It seems that the following development may occur during each day's prayer (five exercises) on a single mystery of Christ's life. At first you may tend to stand outside the mystery, reading and reflecting on the Scriptural event. Then you may use your imagination to see and hear the persons and actions in the mystery. The next step may be to feel yourself actually present at the mystery and even becoming a part of the mystery (as a servant). Finally, as the presence and involvement deepen, you may be carried beyond the externals to an experience of the person or persons present in the mystery. This deeply personal encounter may be an experience of joy, sorrow, goodness, love, justice, and even of «divinity» of the «Other.» Christ's way of uniting himself to us as you contemplate may touch, enter and penetrate even your most human feelings.

CHAPTER 10

THE TWO STANDARDS

This is what you are to teach them to believe and persuade them to do. Anyone who teaches anything different, and does not keep to the sound teaching which is that of our Lord Jesus Christ, the doctrine which is in accordance with true religion, is simply ignorant and must be full of self-conceit — with a craze for questioning everything and arguing about words. All that can come of this is jealousy, contention, abuse and wicked mistrust of one another; and unending disputes by people who are neither rational nor informed and imagine that religion is a way of making a profit. Religion, of course, does bring large profits, but only to those who are content with what they have. We brought nothing into the world, and we can take nothing out of it; but as long as we have food and clothing, let us be content with that. People who long to be rich are a prey to temptation; they get trapped into all sorts of foolish and dangerous ambitions which eventually plunge them into ruin and destruction. 'The love of money is the root of all evils' and there are some who, pursuing it, have wandered away from the faith, and so given their souls any number of fatal wounds.

But, as a man dedicated to God, you must avoid all that. You must aim to be saintly and religious, filled with faith and love, patient and gentle. Fight the good fight of the faith and win for yourself the eternal life to

159

*which you were called when you made your profession
and spoke up for the truth in front of many witnesses.
Now, before God the source of all life and before Jesus
Christ, who spoke up as a witness for the truth in front
of Pontius Pilate, I put to you the duty of doing all that
you have been told. (1 Tm 6:2-13)*

One of my reasons for placing Scriptural texts at the head of each chapter is so that readers may notice that most of the imagery and ideas discussed by Ignatius in the *Exercises* are biblical. When he speaks about the King, he is using not merely medieval but biblical imagery. When he speaks about the war between Christ and Satan, he presents it in military imagery which is also Scriptural. This imagery is very prominent in St. Paul. And when Ignatius speaks about the tactics of the devil in luring people from riches to honors and to pride, the text we have read assures us that this doctrine too is based on Scripture.

In this chapter we will discuss the meditation on the «Two Standards» and its connection with discernment and with spiritual counseling. Ignatius introduces this part of the Exercises by referring to the choice of two states of life already considered when contemplating Christ's hidden life, that is, the state of those who follow the commandments and the life of the evangelical counsels. Ignatius develops this point at once:

While continuing to contemplate His life, let us begin to investigate and ask in what kind of life or in what state His Divine Majesty wishes to make use of us.

Therefore, as some introduction to this, in the next exercise, let us consider the intention of Christ our Lord, and on the other hand, that of the enemy of our human nature. Let us also see how we ought to prepare ourselves to arrive at perfection in whatever state or way of life God our Lord may grant us to choose. [135]

A whole day is to be spent on the meditation on «Two Standards» and on «Three Classes of Men» before continuing the contemplation of Christ's public life. We might call it a day of introduction. Through the exercises on «Two Standards,» «Three Classes of Men» and «Three Kinds of Humility,» Ignatius hopes to induce in retreatants the right dispositions for choosing well.

At the same time various factors bearing on the decision to be made should be brought together. If it is a question of choosing a state of life, then one begins to weigh the choice immediately. Still, at this point the emphasis should remain on dispositions. The three meditations, the «Two Standards,» the «Three Classes of Men» and the «Three Kinds of Humility,» are meant to dispose the person to recognize the Lord's will when it is made known.

The meditation on the «Two Standards» is intended to provide deeper knowledge of the two leaders and their tactics. We will become familiar with the deceits of our enemy and learn to recognize him «by the trail of evil marking his course.» [334] There is no question, as a number of commentators have noted, of a choice between the standard of Christ and the standard of Satan. Our established desire is to be admitted for life under the standard of Christ. This meditation, then, is not an examination of conscience. Unfortunately, in making the meditation many people are mistakenly led to examine their conscience anew. The aim is rather to understand the deceits of the evil one.

Now, it is usually the case that, when a retreatant is doing this exercise, he begins to understand the deceits of the enemy by looking at some of the devil's actions in his own life. But the purpose of reviewing these actions is not to induce a sense of sorrow or a sense of guilt, but rather to see how the enemy of our human nature has succeeded in influencing him in the past. Similarly, he wishes to know the tactics which Christ our Leader uses to save man and to bring him to the fullness of being. His ultimate purpose, of course, is that he can share in that work with Christ.

This theme of two leaders, of two standards and two cities pervades Christian history and Christian spirituality. It is found, as well, in other spiritualities; it is not something new. Ignatius presents this theme in the baroque mode; this is especially true of the image of Satan. But there are hundreds of texts in the Old and New Testaments describing this struggle between Satan and God to gain the allegiance of, and win over to themselves, the members of the human race.

Ignatius begins with a picture of the two leaders, Satan on a smoky throne near Babylon, terrible to behold, and the peaceful, gentle Christ on a lowly plain outside Jerusalem. Unless they have had a vivid experience of hell, many people will find difficulty with this image of Satan. A common reaction today is that it is unreal. We feel that Satan is a lot more subtle than he is portrayed.

But there are two ways in which Satan confronts a person. At times he is very threatening: he comes at one like that vixen Ignatius describes, or like the general, very forcefully and very directly. His other approach is more subtle. In this vein William Barrett in his *Irrational Man* compares Nietzsche's false, grandiose devil with Dostoevski's petty, paltry, mean devil in the person of Ivan in *The Brothers Karamazov*.

The devil presents himself in many different guises. But it is good to remember that the terrifying presentation of Satan on his throne surrounded by smoke and fire is all sham. Satan has no power whatsoever — beyond his capacity to fill men with fear. And here Ignatius pictures the Satan who approaches a man filled with fear.

Sometime or other in his life everyone has been overcome by fright. One of Satan's main tactics is to inspire fear. The more subtle approach of Satan, on the other hand, is the innuendo, the sneaky little temptations by which he manoeuvers men without their knowing it. And, of course, the frightening aspect of Satan stands in contrast with the gentle, loving Christ who brings peace and quiet and confidence.

Ignatius then presents the figure of Christ, our true leader, and reveals his program. Christ stands among his disciples and his apostles, and he sends them throughout the world. It appears to be an unequal warfare: on one side is the devil with all the advantages on his side; over against him are the human creatures Christ chooses. The counterpart of the devils might have been guardian angels, but Ignatius has not presented it that way. He prefers to show the incarnate Son speaking familiarly with his humble followers:

> Consider the address which Christ our Lord makes to all His servants and friends whom he sends on this enterprise, recommending to them to seek to help all, first by attracting them to the highest spiritual poverty, and should it please the Divine Majesty, and should He deign to choose them for it, even to actual poverty. Secondly, they should lead them to a desire for insults and contempt, for from these spring humility. [146]

Ignatius next describes the programs of the two leaders. Satan's is to enslave men, to turn them in on themselves, to make them self-centered, to get them involved in their own egotisms. No single individual of any state in life is overlooked: Satan wages a war that involves the whole universe. His intention is to reduce men to slavery and thus prevent them from reaching their completion and fulfillment. He tends to emphasize the soft way, the easy way, that which caters to man's concupiscence. Thus, his program runs as follows: «First they are to tempt them to covet riches (as Satan himself is accustomed to do in most cases) that they may the more easily attain the empty honors of this world, and then come to overweening pride.» [142] The emptiness of the honors sought is inserted here by Ignatius. The desire for those honors can be very great, but the honors themselves are in fact empty.

Satan's technique is always to exaggerate. He exaggerates the natural tendencies of the individual, even those which are most legitimate. Since he is the «father of lies,» he lies both by understatement and by overstatement. For example, he will take your talents and exaggerate them until he has trapped you in pride. He can then do anything with you. Once pride has taken hold, you will commit crimes to retain your position: kill people, start wars — anything.

Or Satan will take a man's weaknesses and exaggerate them to stir up self-pity. Then the person's whole life is disturbed. He goes around filled with self-pity, complaining that nobody loves him and that the community itself is not loving. Such self-pity can affect a person deeply impinging even on his body and showing itself in his looks and carriage.

Christ's approach is the opposite of Satan's. He is the way, the truth and the life; honesty, openness, and genuineness mark his approach. He urges us to accept the talents we have been given. Instead of exaggerating their importance to the point of pride, Christ leads us to thank the Father and recognize them as the gifts of the Father.

164

In other words, he doesn't say «You have no talents.» That would be a lie: each of us has been given gifts and talents. Instead, Christ says, «Attribute them to their source.» As the retreatant will discover in the «Contemplation to Attain Love of God,» all gifts come from one supreme Giver. Accordingly, Christ says, «Be thankful, be grateful to the Lord for the talents he has given you.»

On the other hand, to the person who experiences weakness he counsels, «You are right, but the weak things of the world God has chosen to confound the strong.» And the individual is consoled by the realization that God uses him through his weaknesses. Amazingly enough, often that is precisely the way God seems to use us best.

In this meditation we are not asked to choose between the two parties or their two platforms; rather, we seek to understand how we can serve Jesus Christ. How can we be with Christ, working for the redemption of the world? It draws us back again to the «Call of the King» and deepens our sense of what the commitment involves.

The programs of Satan and of Christ may help the exercitant to realize how he relates to things in terms of riches or poverty? Does he see them as something to be grasped or something to be appreciated? Does he see them as gifts of the Father? What is his relationship with other people? Does he look for honors from them or for the truth? Does he approach them with a desire to overpower them, to have them look up to him, to accord him empty praise? Or does he approach them as though he knew them to be better than himself, all sons and daughters of the Father? And as far as he himself is concerned, how does he look upon himself, in pride or in humility? Does he relate to himself proudly as he thinks of his own achievements? Or is he cast down by an excessive sense of helplessness?

The puritan ethic of achievement has had a profound effect on Roman Catholics living in an Anglo-Saxon culture. In this ethic thriftiness, hard work, and financial security are signs of goodness, signs of the elect. It maintains that certain people have been elected by God for salvation and that one of the signs of election is a man's success in this world. His prosperity on earth means that he is one of God's chosen ones — provided he is not a murderer, adulterer, or thief. This ethic pervades our culture to the extent that many people consider poverty to be the poor man's own fault. In short, the puritan ethic makes it difficult for us to accept the truth that money and honor are means of overweening pride. Its broad assumptions have been in possession for four or five generations now, but in the last ten to twenty years our culture has been moving away from it. To some extent, at least, contrary views have been gaining ground.

The program of Christ makes strong demands on his followers: «Hence, there will be three steps: the first, poverty as opposed to riches; the second, insults or contempt as opposed to the honor of this world; the third, humility as opposed to pride. From these three steps, let them lead men to all other virtues.» [146] It is not easy to persuade anyone to choose the true way when it involves difficulty, nor would the Madison Avenue adman ever espouse that cause. To believe that a difficult course is the way to freedom is often repugnant to one's natural tendencies. But that is exactly what Christ challenges men to accept.

In his book, *Poverty of Spirit* [14], Metz lists six or seven experiences of poverty: poverty of the commonplace, poverty of misery and neediness, the poverty of uniqueness and superiority from which comes responsibility, poverty of one's provisional nature as a human being (man's creatureliness), poverty

166

of his finiteness. These may help the retreatant to understand the phrase, «highest spiritual poverty.»

There is the poverty of creaturehood, «Blessed are those who feel the need of God.» There is the poverty of sinfulness: not only are men poor as creatures, but they are even poorer because of their sins. There is the poverty in one's Christian vocation, the awareness a man has that he is not worthy, that he has been called to something that is beyond him — to serve with Christ. Genuine love makes him poor.

Every genuine human encounter must be inspired by poverty of spirit. When one is truly meeting someone else, he approaches the other on his knees. Paul advises him: «Always consider the other person to be better than yourself.» (Ph 2:3) There is nothing forced or insincere about such an attitude; it is genuine humility. It recognizes that the other person is a child of God, loved by the Father, and in some way superior to oneself.

Christ is the great example of poverty. He is the one who is poor in spirit. You notice in his program that Christ says, «attracting them to the highest spiritual poverty, and should it please the Divine Majesty, and should He deign to choose them for it, even to actual poverty.» [146] Actual poverty is a kind of test of genuineness of spiritual poverty. It tests a man's honesty in seeking the highest spiritual poverty.

«Secondly, they should lead them to a desire for insults and contempt, for from these springs humility.» [146] I mentioned already what I call the active acceptance of suffering, versus the merely passive way. Notice that Ignatius uses the word «desire» here, while later in the «Triple Colloquy» he speaks, not of «desiring,» but of «bearing» insults and wrongs. At the moment of being called to his standard, Christ wants his followers to desire insults and contempt. There is quite a difference between desiring insults and bearing them when they come. Believers can deceive themselves into thinking that they can bear insults. Christ goes beyond this to urge the Christian even to desire them.

To be a Christian means, in great part, to have some degree of spiritual poverty. Hence, the retreatant's request for spiritual poverty in the «Triple Colloquy» can be absolute, and he can ask that it be given him in the highest degree: «Blessed are the poor in spirit.» But when he asks for actual poverty, his request is conditioned by his acceptance of God's designs in the concrete details of his life, that is, if God wants him to live a life of actual poverty. Ignatius says, «should the Divine Majesty be pleased thereby, and deign to choose and accept me, even in actual poverty; secondly, in bearing insults and wrongs, thereby to imitate him better, provided only I can suffer these without sin on the part of another, and without offense of the Divine Majesty. Then I will say the *Hail Mary*.» [147] The retreatant goes to our Lady asking her to make this request of her son, and then to the Son and asks him to beg this of the Father. Ignatius instructs him to make this exercise four times on the same day. The exercise on «Three Classes of Men» is to be the fifth; it is made in place of the «Application of the Senses» as a practical, concrete application of the meditation on «Two Standards.»

The program of Christ is indeed a difficult one for weak human beings to face. Ignatius shifts from a consideration of what is «out there» to one which focuses on the retreatant's own interior needs. He is to be a disciple of Christ and to present Christ's program to others, but in the «Triple Colloquy» he discovers that this program is for himself as well as for others. He is to be with Christ his king evangelizing other people, but he discovers that he cannot urge others to submit to these demands unless he is willing to accept them himself. In the «Triple Colloquy» this shift to his own needs takes place. In our Lady he finds all that is humanly good responding totally to God. So he seeks the support of the whole human community, whose goodness is focused in her person.

Often after a person first makes this meditation, he will remark that he has no real problem in asking for actual poverty. But when the conditions of actual poverty are described in concrete terms, such as no daily showers, no soap, and sleeping on the ground, then he may begin to realize that even to desire actual poverty is a grace. In religious communities today, people tend to romanticize actual poverty, not realizing what it is in reality.

Someone might question whether there can really be a call to actual poverty today. I feel we have to answer, «Yes, there can.» There are men and women on the missions in Canada and Asia who are living in severe poverty. But not necessarily the poverty of the people they serve. Their physical constitution cannot operate in such poverty. And there are men and women in religious communities who have not only felt the call but really live in actual poverty. There are the Little Brothers and Sisters of Jesus. It is not impossible; rather, the question is whether some members of the community actually experience this call. For it is certainly a call.

Now, this is a genuine concern of religious life today, but that is not the point of the meditation. The meditation is to be seen in relation to the choice of a state of life. There are a number of points to the meditation, but I suppose that the basic one is freedom with Christ. The question of freedom comes up again in the exercise on «Three Classes of Men.» Still, it is important to open oneself to the possibility that one might be called to actual poverty.

This is quite different from the question of the vow of poverty as it is being lived in religious communities. Religious

169

communities have to be open to the possibility that some among them are really being called to this kind of actual poverty, and they should encourage those who are called to it. Poverty and discernment go together, especially from a community viewpoint. But an apostolate has a number of dimensions to it. It has the dimension of service and witness, as well as that of actual poverty.

When presenting this meditation, it is good to give some examples of what actual poverty is. This lends realism to the prayer and makes it a real exercise. Otherwise, the exercitant might say to himself, «I have no trouble with actual poverty. What I find difficult is the bearing of insults and wrong.»

The poverty — riches contrast has to do with things such as money, material things, university degrees, personality, the whole range of personal talents. What are a man's riches, the things in which he finds security? He may need to have a degree for apostolic reasons, but it may also be for the honor involved. The devil uses all such riches to ensnare a person.

One of the purposes of the meditation is that the exercitant should come to understand how Satan operates in him, should discern the techniques of the evil one. Probably the focal point is the question of honors and dishonors, because these are strong motives. He is to be exercised, and the exercising is also a kind of exorcising: it is in this type of exercise that he is being exorcised of fears that dominate him. He is brought face to face with the very thing he is fearful of, and he is made free by grace. A man's need to be accepted is valid. This and many other needs may be good. The main point is to know when he is ensnared by them and when he is free. Our need for affection, too, is a valid need, but when that becomes exaggerated, we can lose our freedom.

«The first step, then, will be riches, the second honor, the third pride. From these three steps the evil one leads to all other vices.» [142] Once a man is proud, once he thinks he is self-sufficient, he can be led to do anything. Most detective stories describe persons who become so enslaved with themselves that killing someone else seems insignificant to them. And we know that there are those who have given themselves over to evil. Whether they have done it intentionally or not is another question: we cannot make such moral judgments. But we do see that they get to such a state of mind, they become so taken up with themselves, that they can kill without any qualms of conscience.

To understand the difference between the two leaders one has to investigate more thoroughly what is meant by «riches, honor, and pride.» One young person told me recently that it was just the opposite with him: his real temptation was to look down his nose at the rich and their possessions. He had recognized in himself the fact that his reaction against affluence could take the form of pride. But this special development among some members of the younger generation is not actually different from what Ignatius has proposed as the pattern of vice. What this young man had realized was that, in his own subculture at least, Satan could lead him to another kind of honor and pride.

The first step towards pride is always the pursuit of «riches,» and riches normally mean some form of material wealth or possessions. But not always, because the meaning of any individual's «riches» will depend upon what tends to bring him «honor.» In today's world, I suppose, honors mean being accepted or being respected within one's own subculture. As Ignatius presents riches, they should be understood as whatever gives a particular person the sense of being honored: clothes, house, car, popularity, academic degrees, admiration, positions of power, success with this or that group.

If we try to understand this being whom we call «Satan»

or «the devil,» we come to see him as the force of evil that moves in on us from outside, as the destructive force in a subculture that plays havoc with teenagers and minority groups just as much as the evil tendencies in the main culture that influence most of us all the time. Certain currents in a subculture may powerfully shape the attitudes of a teenager, a slum-dweller, or a wealthy executive, and drifts of opinion, unexamined assumptions on a national scale, and new social developments may form the very soul of those in the cultural mainstream. Satan adapts himself to all of these trends. His malign influence exerts a personally destructive effect on us from outside ourselves. And just as another person can mysteriously change us, this outside force moves in on us without our noticing where it may lead; it communicates its suggestive power non-verbally to our inner selves.

One danger is that the director may too quickly judge the exercitant to be filled with pride. You cannot easily know that conclusion. You will have to wait and see. The fact a person says he is filled with pride does not end the process of discernment. It is important to know where his trouble is coming from. How is pride working in his life? Often you will find that there is a dimension that is not pride itself. Perhaps it may be a pelagian approach or a perfectionist tendency, or maybe fear is operating.

It is often necessary to wait, to be patient, and not to jump to conclusions. It is not always wise to agree, «Well, yes, you're filled with pride.» Sometimes this can be done as a shock technique, but you should be very careful with methods of that sort. Normally, even though you think you have spotted the pattern of a person's life, it is better to let him find it out for himself. It is far better for the Spirit to lead the individual to deeper self-understanding. The Spirit will certainly do so when the person is ready.

172

Matthew's version of the *Our Father* ends with «Deliver us from the evil one.» I believe it was Bonhoeffer who said that the words, «Deliver us from the evil one,» mean «Do not let us think that we can go it alone.» The big temptation is to think that we can get through life without God, or that the human race as a whole can achieve fulfillment without turning to its Creator and Father.

Films sometimes help to make people aware of the presence of evil in our world. In addition, many books and articles published in recent years take account of the evil dimension as it assails individuals. In *Love and Will,* for example, Rollo May speaks about the demonic in our culture. But most people are already conscious that the world is disordered and chaotic. Some sections of the younger generation react strongly against older institutions because they feel that certain social and cultural structures are expressions of evil, built into our civilization, that tend to oppress and destroy them from outside themselves. Others may look at the problem in an opposite way, but most of the parties in contention, whatever their various explanations, agree about the presence of external evil itself.

Evil forces, however, are internal as well. There are also disorders within us that escape our control: «The things that I would, I do not.» (Rm 7:19) We need not look far abroad because much of the trouble is right at home.

But whether it is coming from outside or from inside, the effect is the same: I become preoccupied with myself, with the oppressions that surround me and the disorders within me. And that is a form of egotism and pride. On the other hand, Christ's influence tends to move me beyond myself. Bonhoeffer calls Christ «The man for others.» Satan's desire is to turn me in on myself to the extent that I become enslaved and become a destructive force in this universe. The thrust from Christ is the

173

opposite, to enhance my freedom so that I become a creative force of love. It is the spirit of self-centeredness and selfishness versus the spirit of openness and self-sacrifice for the good of others.

In the «Two Standards» Ignatius says that poverty and humiliations are the means to humility. But another powerful means to humility is the experience of being loved. At the beginning of the Exercises it is important for the retreatant to experience the love of God in some measure before he considers sin, he may find himself open to a new love. And it is through the gift of God's love that the experience of a deeper humility becomes possible.

The same is true in human love as well. One who falls in love becomes humble in the face of another's gift of self. The gift stirs up deep gratitude and with it the desire to serve and to give oneself in return. This is exactly what happens when the Father sends his Son to us, when the Spirit leads us in prayer to open our hearts to Christ, and when Jesus himself reveals his personal love and understanding of our condition.

This meditation reinforces the strategy of the Trinity and the program of Christ already introduced in the contemplations on the hidden life. But in the «Two Standards» Ignatius presents these more starkly by introducing the enemy of mankind, Satan, and his program. Because Ignatius knows that the truths he is presenting are difficult to accept, five meditations are given to this subject — the «Three Classes of Men» is a variation on the theme.

Moreover, the «Triple Colloquy» is continued throughout the rest of the «Second Week» and even in the «Third Week.» [159, 161, 199] One benefit that this prayer to our Lady, our Lord, and the Father can bring is true appreciation of the beatitudes. One begins to realize that poverty of spirit, meekness, gentleness, kindness, desire for peace and justice are graces, as is suffering for the name of Jesus. They are blessings from the Lord that one can only pray for and be grateful to receive. But when they are experienced, what freedom and peace they bring! — the freedom and peace of Christ's kingdom: «How blessed are the poor in spirit; theirs is the kingdom of heaven.» (Mt 5:3)

CHAPTER 11

THREE CLASSES AND THREE KINDS

A member of one of the leading families put this question to him, 'Good Master, what have I to do to inherit eternal life?' Jesus said to him, 'Why do you call me good? No one is good but God alone. You know the commandments: You must not commit adultery; You must not kill; You must not steal; You must not bring false witness; Honor your father and mother.' *He replied, 'I have kept all these from my earliest days till now.' And when Jesus heard this he said, 'There is still one thing you lack. Sell all that you own and distribute the money to the poor, and you will have treasure in heaven; then come, follow me.' But when he heard this he was filled with sadness, for he was very rich.*

Jesus looked at him and said, 'How hard it is for those who have riches to make their way into the kingdom of God! Yes, it is easier for a camel to pass through the eye of a needle than for a rich man to enter the kingdom of God.' 'In that case' said the listeners 'who can be saved?' 'Things that are impossible for men' he replied 'are possible for God.'

Then Peter said, 'What about us? We left all we had to follow you.' He said to them, 'I tell you solemnly, there is no one who has left house, wife, brother, parents or children for the sake of the kingdom of God who will not be given repayment many times over in this present time and, in the world to come, eternal life.' (Lk 18:18-30)

I cannot help but smile when I read this passage because the listeners' question: «Who can be saved?», reminds me of the puritan ethic. If a rich man cannot get into heaven, who can? The assumptions that lurk behind their perplexity are worth considering — especially today.

Against those silent assumptions Ignatius aims the «Three Classes of Men.» I have already noted that this meditation is to be made on the same day of the «Second Week,» the same day as the meditation on «Two Standards.» Once again, we will consider this meditation from the viewpoint of freedom.

There are some interesting points to consider in Ignatius's text. The first thing to notice is that the men involved have received a large sum of money honestly — for example, by way of an inheritance. It has not been gained through criminal action. Yet they fear losing their souls by becoming attached to their riches. «Each of them has acquired ten thousand ducats, but not entirely as they should have, for the love of God. They all wish to save their souls and find peace in God our Lord by ridding themselves of the burden arising from the attachment to the sum acquired, which impedes the attainment of this end.» [150] They know the passage in Luke quoted above, which affirms that «It is easier for a camel to pass through the eye of a needle than for a rich man to enter the kingdom of God.» The «eye of a needle» may refer to the little door in the large gate of an Eastern city. Camels could not get through this door but a man could.

While praying for the grace to choose the *magis:* «to choose what is more for the glory of His Divine Majesty and the salvation of my soul,» [152] the exercitant is to consider the different reactions of the three groups of men.

Let us look more closely at these three groups. The men of the first class want to get rid of the attachment, but, like Hamlet, they procrastinate until somebody puts poison in their drink.

Those of the second class rationalize their way. This meditation impressed me deeply about three years ago when a number of novices, both men and women openly placed themselves with this second class. They realized that their entry into religious life had only the semblance of an offering of themselves to the community since it was on their own conditions. They had entered saying, «I'll enter and I'll try it out; but I'll stay only if everything agrees with me.»

The men of the third class are in quite a paradoxical position because they do not actually give up the money. The money remains in their possession, but they are detached from it; they stand aside from it. Although the grace being sought is «to choose what is more for the glory of His Divine Majesty and the salvation of my soul,» [152] the purpose of the meditation is to attain a disposition of indifference and detachment. In other words, the grace to choose what is more for the glory of God is a choice that affects one's disposition rather than a choice that concerns some specific use of things. At the end of the meditation Ignatius tells us to use the same three colloquies assigned in the «Two Standards.»

The way I usually present this meditation is to describe the first group of men as those who put money in the bank and leave it there. They ponder the fact that they are rich and should do something about their responsibility, but nothing ever comes of it. They do not want to get rid of this possession. The second group are like men determined to face a hard decision. They are men of action, but they want to maintain control. They «get rid» of this money by building a library or a hospital and putting their name in neon lights: «The Brown Brothers Memorial Hospital.» They keep the honor and the glory that come from a splendid benefaction. And the third group are like men who might set up a trust fund for refugee relief or for some other

178

good cause. They are still waiting for an indication of how they should apply the trust fund; meanwhile, they have set the money aside.

Keeping this in mind, let us return to the grace we are to seek. It is very enigmatic. Ignatius does not say that the retreatant should seek the grace to belong to the third class of men. Rather he suggests that the retreatant pray «to choose what is more for the glory of His Divine Majesty and the salvation of [his] soul.» [152] It is the «more» (*magis*) indicated in the «Principle and Foundation,» the choice of whatever will better serve God our Lord. It is an interesting grace to ask for. Notice that the men of the third class do not exactly decide on a course of action, but rather they desire to be better able to serve God our Lord; that desire alone is to be «the cause of their accepting anything or relinquishing it.» [155]

Indifference is what the meditation is all about. Contrary to the impression one might receive from a first reading, the meditation does not deal with any definite use of creatures. Instead, Ignatius is testing the retreatant's indifference. He wants him to achieve a freedom from things that will allow him to attach himself totally to God and to his service.

Perhaps I may be permitted at this point to use a rather homely illustration — one taken from my own experience in making this meditation. I was in Wales for my final year of training in the Jesuit Order, and this included a thirty-day retreat. While praying over the «Three Classes of Men,» I looked around my simply furnished room and examined the contents of my trunk, the few books on my shelf, my clothing. There seemed to be nothing much that I could not cheerfully part with. What about the typewriter I had been given at my Ordination? — such a gift was unusual in those days. After some hesitation, I felt at peace there too. It could go with the rest.

179

But then my eyes fell on a small filing cabinet filled with the notes I had compiled during the previous twelve years. I must say that I had quite a time with that set of files. I felt a clutch of fear and insecurity: what if I were to fly back from England, but shipped the files home in my trunk and the boat sank on the way? My whole life's work, all nicely filed and sorted, would go down with that ship. How could I, a young priest, give sermons and talks up and down the land if I were deprived of my precious resources? It may seem ridiculous now, but if the house had been on fire, I would have risked flames and smoke to save that treasure.

Somehow or other I had based too much of my trust for the future upon the results of my own labor — to the extent that I experienced serious dismay at the mere thought of losing a set of notes. When in my prayer I realized this foolishness clearly, and struggled to get rid of my burden, what a tremendous experience of freedom came to me! With a sense of real joy I accepted the fact that the Lord could work in me, could achieve whatever he wanted, without any notes at all. I would try to place all my confidence in him alone.

It is something of this nature that we consider in the «Three Classes of Men.» What in my life is enslaving me? What is interfering with my freedom and with a total offering of myself to God?

The meditation on «Three Classes» is a practical application of Christ's program of love and responsibility. The retreatant moves away from insecurity, fear, and self-love towards detachment from all things and attachment only to God's will. The meditation becomes, then, an occasion for him to examine his conscience on whatever might be standing as a block to his openness to the Spirit of God who desires to make himself known.

How can such blocks be recognized? The particular call of conscience in the midst of temptation often clarifies the source of opposition in each individual. Man's conscience is the voice of transcendence: he may interpret the voice, but he does not originate it. And, at least insofar as temptation comes to him from the evil that is external to him and all around him, every man is like Jesus.

Jesus was tempted, as other men are, to refuse his responsibility in the form of life to which he was being led by the Spirit. Usually, at such moments in a man's life, there is one thing that threatens to dominate him. It may be fear that holds him back, or ambition that egotistically drives him forward, or pride that makes him want to enslave others to himself. But at the moment of temptation a person must make a choice: conscience calls him one way, and blocking forces rise up to prevent that movement from being realized. Only through union with the Lord, the source of freeing love can he break through the wall of opposition and gain true freedom.

Inordinate attachments in the proper sense, can be directed only towards things as distinct from persons. But since persons (in denial of their very personhood) can be regarded and used as things, persons can in fact enter into consideration in this meditation where Ignatius tests my disposition toward things. Indeed, much prayer and reflection is needed to see if one is treating the persons in one's life as though they were things.

If a man treats persons as things, then he can ask the Lord to separate him from that person. Since this can be an extremely hard prayer to make, it may require time. The note added at the end of the meditation, [157] like the «Triple Colloquy,» continues to have pertinence through the rest of the «Second Week,» and, if necessary, through the «Third Week.» Consider in particular the following sentence: «We should insist that we desire it [actual poverty], beg for it, plead for it, provided, of course, that it be for the service and praise of the Divine Goodness.» [157]

Attachment to a person of the opposite sex may not be a call to marriage but only a sign of inordinate need. You sometimes discover with novices, for example, that their desire to go home comes more from loneliness than from love. So you try to help them to face the loneliness. Or they feel they are not accepted by the group, so you try to correct that impression.

The Lord says bluntly, «If any man comes to me without hating his father, mother, wife, children, brothers, sisters, yes and his own life too, he cannot be my disciple.» (Lk 14:26) He demands that kind of dedication from us. In other places in the gospels Christ insists that we love the brethren. But the «thing» dimension in an individual's relationship with his parents, for example, may have to be hated for Christ's sake. What you must do is to separate out the «thingness» in order to help the person become free of it in the interpersonal relationship.

Now, obviously, if you are directing someone and he is dominated by attachments to another person, you really have to ask the question: «Has this individual a vocation to the religious life?» If he feels convinced that he has such a vocation and if this conviction is verified by other signs and consolations, you keep encouraging him to pray that the inordinate attachment may be removed. But if the inordinate attachment does not go, then it may be an ordered attachment and the person has no vocation to the religious life but one to the married state.

In the note at the end of the meditation, already mentioned, [157] Ignatius gives an added direction. The person is to pray over whatever in his life is hindering him from totally surrendering to the Lord. Of course, it sometimes takes quite a while for the person to find out what that hindrance is. At other times it will stand out at once and he will be very conscious what it is.

When a person is praying over his vocation, he can easily lapse into romanticism. Ignatius forestalls this weakness by having him make a specific demand on himself in order to root out what is holding him back. It may be nothing more than some material possession that is dominating him. Classically, Ignatius's approach is known as the *agere contra* — «to go against oneself.» The principle of the *agere contra* was for a long time a prominent feature of ascetical training. It can be misused, but Ignatius uses it rightly here. He advises one who feels inordinately attached to something to ask the Lord to remove it or to give him the very opposite.

The example Ignatius uses is poverty, «when we feel an attachment opposed to actual poverty... to beg our Lord in the colloquies to choose us to serve Him in actual poverty.» [157] The *agere contra* is intended to effect a change within the person himself and not necessarily in the objective situation. He prays, in contradiction to his natural desires and inclinations, that the Lord will remove the desired object if that be his will. But to remove it may not be, in fact, the will of the Lord. Someone once asked me, «What happened to those notes of yours?» I still have them. Through the grace of prayer, I possess them in freedom.

I mentioned very early in these pages that determining the will of God is not the more difficult thing. The more difficult thing is to become free of inordinate attachments so that the will of God may be manifest. This is especially true when, in the «Second Week», we are desirous to choose the better and are not limiting ourselves to good over evil. Inordinate attachments do more than inhibit us from acting; they tend to narrow our vision and becloud our perceptions so that it becomes difficult if not impossible for us to discern God's will, especially when there is danger that we might be called upon to give up the object of the attachment.

Hence, the *agere contra* is often used by God as an occasion for giving this grace of freedom. A moment comes in your prayer when you experience this freedom. You know it is a grace from the Lord because it is beyond, and perhaps contrary to, your natural inclination. It is an uplifting experience of the freedom of the sons of God.

The term «actual poverty» does include all material goods but it may be extended to other possessions. One's «riches» are those things apart from Christ in which one finds one's security — even the status of priesthood, religious life or university professor, a husband, a wife. So in this exercise Ignatius urges the retreatant to identify his «riches» and to ask the Lord to remove them. Such a prayer may be answered literally. On the other hand the person may gain an indifference to his riches. He may then be able to appreciate these things, honors, and talents, as gifts rather than as «riches.»

The meditation on the «Three Classes of Men» gives the antecedent dispositions required of one who wishes to be accepted under Christ's standard. Such a person quite naturally moves to a more active offering of self much as Ignatius expresses it in the «Three Kinds of Humility,» to which I now turn.

The following words of St. Paul encourage one to consider Ignatius's treatment of the «Three Kinds of Humility» [165-8] and to seek the graces needed:

> I was given a thorn in the flesh, an angel of Satan to beat me and stop me from getting too proud! About this thing, I have pleaded with the Lord three times for it to leave me, but he said, 'My grace is enough for you: my power is at its best in weakness'. So I shall be very happy to make my weaknesses my special boast so that the power of Christ may stay over me, and that is why I

184

am quite content with my weaknesses, and with insults, hardships, persecutions, and the agonies I go through for Christ's sake. For it is when I am weak that I am strong.
(2 Co 12:7-10)

Ignatius writes in concrete fashion of mortal and venial sin in order to give us a framework within which to locate the various kinds of humility. The first kind is expressed in these words: «I subject and humble myself [so] as to obey the law of God.» [165] Ignatius does not speak of desires and attitudes here because this humility is necessary for salvation. But in the second and third kinds he speaks of «my attitude of mind» [166] and says that «I desire and choose poverty with Christ poor,... I desire to be accounted as worthless and a fool for Christ.» [167] These words indicate that the purpose of the consideration is to seek a new attitude of soul, a new relationship to Christ.

The retreatant is asked to consider, not his personal history of sin, but rather his attitude toward Christ. It may be that he would not want to commit a mortal sin, that he would not want to commit a venial sin, or that he would want to suffer with Christ. This is not to say that he does not sin venially or mortally. For this, after all, is dependent on his cooperation with grace. In fact, what usually happens is that, the more that one wants to love Christ and to suffer with him, the more conscious he becomes that he is imperfect, that he is a sinner. This consideration, then, is not a question of not sinning; it is a question of attitude, of desire.

I mentioned that the «Three Classes of Men» deal primarily with our relations with things. I would say that the «Three Kinds of Humility» are concerned with our relations with persons, in particular the person of Christ. Since we cannot divide Christ, this relation extends to all human persons. Our desire is to be totally influenced by Jesus Christ, and to be concerned with the personhood of another rather than with his talents or his other gifts.

With this in mind I would suggest that one way to understand the «Three Kinds of Humility,» or three «modes» of humility, is to consider how they would operate in the relationship between a husband and wife. In some ways, the modes of humility apply better to the wife than to the husband. But let's approach them from the viewpoint of the husband.

In the first mode of humility his approach to his wife is, «I will always be faithful to her to the extent of never committing adultery.» That is a negative expression of what he is trying to say; we often use a negative expression in order to describe a positive reality. He says, in effect, that he will always be faithful to his wife. The point is not the faithfulness itself but the love relationship with the wife. In other words, the husband makes the commitment to love her in such a way as to remain faithful to her and never commit adultery. It does not mean he may not in fact commit adultery on some occasion. He may commit adultery; but his love relationship is of such a nature that, if he does, he will deeply regret it.

In the second mode of humility he would speak about his love as follows: «I will avoid all disturbances with my wife, in the sense that I will always try to be at peace with her and try to be an instrument of peace within the family.»

In the third mode of humility he relates to his wife in this way: «I will feel with her, I will suffer with her in her sufferings, I will be joyful with her in her joy.» Clearly, it will not always be easy to suffer with her in her sufferings. For this reason Ignatius proposes suffering as a test of love. He does not mean that a Christian should not be joyful, but that the acid test of humility and of your sharing with another will be found in suffering.

These «Three Kinds of Humility,» then, represent an expan-

186

sion of the freedom that comes with grace and with the desire to be with Christ and to suffer with Christ. The preposition «with» is very important in the third mode of humility. The accent is not on suffering but on being *with* Christ poor, *with* Christ insulted. This can become the deepest desire in one's being under the urging of the Spirit.

But a man's weak human nature imagines all sorts of humiliations attendant on poverty and dishonor. He forgets that they are to be borne in company with Christ. While you are giving spiritual direction, therefore, great patience and great persistence are needed to help others attain this freedom. You should stay with them until they can abandon themselves and make the full offering of themselves to and with Christ.

This surrender is an act of freedom flowing from trust, and it is expressed very forcefully here in the «Three Kinds of Humility.» With grace this consideration should enable a person to grow in freedom and love. As he is contemplating the life of Christ in the light of the «Three Kinds of Humility,» he will usually undergo movements from the good and evil spirits. This should be expected because in striving to advance he has opened himself up to a new kind of life. He has broken through the initial barriers built by egotism and pride, and he has taken his first steps forward, but he has not yet found his feet. He has not, of course, received the habit of union with Christ. He is drawn to it, he longs to abandon himself totally to the Lord, but he must learn to walk steadily without the old supports.

I remember one person saying to me about the prayer, «Take and Receive,» in the «Contemplation to Attain Love of God»: «That's some prayer. I offer my memory, my understanding, my entire will to God. I ask him to give me only his love and his grace; this will be enough for me. That's some contrast isn't it? I give him my little wee things, and he has to give me the totality of his being.»

187

When the Lord is there, it is easy, but when a person is experiencing suffering and dishonor, usually the Lord does not seem to be there, and it is hard. Some authorities on John Brebeuf have suggested that he was in ecstasy while being martyred. It must have been easier for him than for Gabriel Lalement, who was merely watching. But God gave both of them the strength to suffer and die *with* Christ.

Quite often people fully grasp the third mode of humility only in the «Third Week» when they are praying on the passion. Still, Ignatius places it in the «Second Week.» I think he does this so as to help free the exercitant for the movement of spirits and for the discerning process that is to come. The «Third Week» exercises constitute a confirmation of the decision.

We pray on the passion in order to see whether the decision we made in the «Second Week» is what the Lord wants. We check it out against the passion of Christ. Union with Christ suffering will normally be the time of clearer discernment. It is very easy to be deluded when one is experiencing joy. Discernment is usually verified in the face of suffering.

Spiritual writers say that the second mode of humility is adequate for discernment and for decision making. But when you are directing people, it is important that they come at least to the desire of the third mode. They have to agree in principle with the third mode.

Sometimes a pretentious rational argument develops, e.g., «It's unnatural to want to suffer.» About the only thing you can do to counter this argument is to give them Scripture. Perhaps they will more easily accept Scriptural indications. Then they may accept the principle rationally and intellectually, but they will say they cannot pray to be in the third mode.

So you ask them, «Do you think you should pray for this? Do you think it would be a good thing if you could pray for it?»

In this way they can be led to the desire for the third mode of humility. Even the desire for it brings freedom. If they can say, «Yes, I should desire,» that in itself will liberate them enough for the operations of consolation and desolation to occur. Then the director might present some very difficult situations and ask them if they can live these with the Lord. Often they will say, «Well as long as the Lord's there, I can do it.» And so we can when we are *with* Christ.

These «Three Kinds of Humility» have to do with disposition and not with choice. You hear the expression: «He's choosing according to the third mode of humility.» This indicates a confusion between the *agere contra* practice, by which one acts against his inclination as a method of attaining freedom, and the disposition of the third mode of humility, which is an attitude of heart in my personal relationship with Christ.

To what extent am I dominated by Christ? How much would I like to be dominated by Christ? A man asks these questions of himself in seeking to achieve a certain disposition and attitude; the choice will be made by God. That is the difficult thing for us to realize. He, not I, will make the decision. His grace will urge me to accept his choice, even of things that may bring me suffering and dishonor.

In the third kind of humility the Christian enters into the *kenosis* of Jesus Christ who «emptied himself to assume the condition of a slave.» (Ph 2:7) His desire to suffer with Christ in poverty and humiliations cannot be controlled by himself, cannot be turned into concrete action, since it is dependent on God's will and greater glory. As he prays to be given this kind of humility his attitude towards the Father becomes one of loving abandonment. In his very lack of control over the future, he is united with Christ in *kenosis*. And his prayer to the Father may be that of Paul: «All I want is to know Christ and the power of his resurrection and to share his sufferings by reproducing the pattern of his death.» (Ph 3:10)

189

CHAPTER 12

DISCERNMENT — SECOND WEEK

Everyone moved by the Spirit is a son of God. The spirit you received is not the spirit of slaves bringing fear into your lives again; it is the spirit of sons, and it makes us cry out, 'Abba, Father!' The Spirit himself and our spirit bear united witness that we are children of God. And if we are children we are heirs as well: heirs of God and coheirs with Christ, sharing his suffering so as to share his glory. ...

The Spirit too comes to help us in our weakness. For when we cannot choose words in order to pray properly, the Spirit himself expresses our plea in a way that could never be put into words, and God who knows everything in our hearts knows perfectly well what he means, and that the pleas of the saints expressed by the Spirit are according to the mind of God. (Rm 8:14-17, 26, 27)

An earlier chapter looked at the mere elementary movements that can occur in those who are struggling to achieve spiritual freedom. The subject of the present chapter is more properly the discernment of spirits. Much has been written on this topic and on its various branches — discernment in the Church as a whole, reading the signs of the times, and so forth. But our sole concern here is with personal discernment, the study of movements that take place in an individual in order to discover what God's will is for him.

Ignatius begins these rules with this introduction: «*Further rules for understanding the different movements produced in the soul. They serve for a more accurate discernment of spirits and are more suitable jor the second week.*» [328] Ignatius does not want these rules to be given to someone still in the «First Week» for they «will be harmful, since they deal with matter that is too subtle and advanced for him to understand.» [9] The time to use these rules is when the director «perceives that the exercitant is being assailed and tempted under the appearance of good.» [10]

By the «Second Week» the exercitant has gained some freedom through the purification of the desires arising from his sinful past and has gained a certain spiritual humility. Although these rules are intended for use during the «Second Week» of the Exercises, they pertain only to the person who has been given the graces and freedom of the «First Week» and even the freedom that comes with the graces of the meditation on «Three Classes of Men,» and the consideration of «Three Kinds of Humility.»

In an article on discernment Michael Kyne [8] maintains that very often the problems of religious and priests are not connected with the generous service of God, but actually problems of human maturity, religious education and motivation. They should therefore be treated according to the rules of discernment of the «First Week» because the «Second Week» rules suppose a settled desire to serve and to do God's will in freedom and generosity.

The usual presumption is that, because a man has taken vows or because he has followed his vocation for twenty years or has been successful in the apostolate, he is now indifferent and free. But often the opposite is true. Kyne argues that, in order to be influenced by the Holy Spirit, a man has to give

himself totally to God. He must avail himself of the freedom a-
rising from the desire to be with Christ, which Ignatius calls the
third mode of humility. In such freedom and peace his generosity
may lead him to extraordinary self-sacrifice and love. If a
person's generosity is decreasing, then contentment is a bad
sign, for it may be the false peace that comes from the evil
spirit. If a person's generosity is increasing, then contentment
is a good sign. It is true peace.

There are three good reasons why spiritual direction is
especially useful at this stage. The first is to lessen hidden selfishness even though that hidden selfishness may have a psychological basis. Secondly, there is need for reasonableness since
the leading of the Spirit will not contradict good sense. And
thirdly, the person must try to understand his life in the framework of the whole life of Christ, of the «Kingdom of Christ,»
the «Two Standards,» the passion, the resurrection and the
growth of the Mystical Body. Hence, life within the church and
in union with the church is a norm for discernment.

While the rules for the «First Week» have a continuing
usefulness for all men, the rules of the «Second Week» are
applicable mainly to generous Christians who want to serve
God totally. In that disposition of generosity such a person is
open to receive graces, but he is also liable to deception.

> It is characteristic of God and His Angels, when they act
> upon the soul, to give true happiness and spiritual joy,
> and to banish all the sadness and disturbances which
> are caused by the enemy.
> It is characteristic of the evil one to fight against
> such happiness and consolation by proposing fallacious
> reasonings, subtilties, and continual deceptions.» [329]

The statement of St. Paul in Romans may be sufficient for

our purposes: «The spirit you received is not the spirit of slaves, bringing fear into your lives.» (Rm 8:14) It is the devil, not the good spirit, who brings fear into the lives of generous souls. Before discernment can successfully help a man find God's will for him, he must often return to the questions: «Who am I? Where did I come from?» In his peaceful sense of identity as a redeemed son of the Father, he can learn how to judge the movement of spirits within himself.

The second and eighth rules should be read together:

> God alone can give consolation to the soul without any previous cause. It belongs solely to the Creator to come into a soul, to leave it, to act upon it, to draw it wholly to the love of His Divine Majesty. ... [330]
>
> When consolation is without previous cause, as was said, there can be no deception in it, since it can proceed from God our Lord only. ... [336]

These statements of Ignatius must have originated in his own experience, but they find confirmation in St. Paul's similar statement: «and this hope is not deceptive, because the love of God has been poured into our hearts by the Holy Spirit which has been given us.» (Rm 5:5)

As the eighth rule continues, it becomes evident how difficult it can be to discern properly when such consolations are granted: «At such a time the soul is still fervent and favored with the grace and aftereffects of the consolation which has passed. In this second period the soul frequently forms various resolutions and plans which are not granted directly by God our Lord.» [336] Even when there is consolation without previous cause, one has to be careful to judge correctly what follows in the afterglow.

The next four rules [331-334] emphasize the need to investigate all the elements of an experience of consolation. «If a cause precedes, both the good angel and the evil spirit can give consolation to a soul... . The good angel consoles for the progress of the soul... . The evil spirit consoles for purposes that are contrary.» [331]

The rule which may have the most frequent application is this one: «It is a mark of the evil spirit to assume the appearance of an angel of light. He begins by suggesting thoughts that are suited to a devout soul, and ends by suggesting his own.» [332] One sign of the enemy is that his good suggestions are often far-fetched, especially with beginners.

For example, a person may start thinking about going on difficult missions, or some other extraordinary apostolate — long before he is purified of mortal sin or deep inordinate attachments. His fantasy may start slowly, but it will gradually expand until he imagines himself as a great apostle of Christ, preaching before a stadium filled with people or organizing a great Christian rally. And then distractions begin: «It will take a great team of men to organize, but we will do this and that, and will people ever look up to me and appreciate me and my talents!» It may start with the illusion of great freedom but it will end by limiting his freedom.

In his insidious attack on obedience in religious communities, the enemy represents obedience as irresponsibility or immaturity. «If I'm to be a free and responsible individual then obedience is not important. In fact, it is wrong, so I won't obey.» No doubt you have experienced this sort of deception personally or in the case of other people.

The enemy can use any pretext. For example, he can start this way: «God has given me a responsibility in the world; therefore I have to work.» And so the victim gives himself to work until he becomes no better than a machine. His work ends

194

in anxiety and pelagianism. All ease in his relationship with God is lost. Again, the enemy can attack from the opposite direction. He can suggest the thought: «Well, now, everything is dependent on God, so let's just take it easy.» His prey becomes lazy, wallows in discontent, and abandons all effort in building God's kingdom. He has found a different reason of discontent. One way or another, the enemy takes something that is basically good, exaggerates it and nudges the person towards selfish solutions.

When you are directing a person in prayer, one of the most obvious signs of the evil spirit acting as an angel of light is the way a thought draws your client away from Christ. Often in the «Second and Third Week» of the Exercises a person will begin to consider undertaking some act for the Lord, either a difficult apostolate, or a great act of humility. Soon he gets all caught up in himself by means of thoughts that are otherwise holy and admirable. But the mystery of Christ's life and the presence of Christ himself disappear, and the grace of deep-felt knowledge of Christ or suffering with Christ is forgotten.

The rules of the «Second Week» are not directly concerned with temptations to sin. Rather, they consider how the enemy tries to disturb a generous Christian; how he pulls a man into anxiety and fear, disturbance and disquiet.

François Roustang, in his book, *Growth in the Spirit,*[15] points out that discernment is needed precisely because the enemy makes use of deception to have us seek evil under the appearance of good. The pharisees, for instance, had zeal without perception. Progress in the spiritual life requires spiritual understanding as well as abnegation and the gift of self. That is why Roustang distinguishes two kinds of criteria when it comes to discernment, subjective and objective. The subjective criteria are the affective experiences of disquiet or delight,

195

disturbance or peace. The objective criteria concern values that can be verified outside oneself.

The subjective experience of joy is the principal sign of the presence of Jesus in us. The love which follows raises one's heart to the Most High. Joy and love lead to peace, to rest and to contentment. Satan brings sadness, attraction to base things, and anxiety. It is not only the sadness of the rich young man, but even more the sadness of Judas, which ends in despair and suicide. On the other hand, Satan can cause false joy, and he can afflict a man with sadness when he takes up a cross.

How, then, does one discern? A basic method is to note the final result. Exactly because there is such a thing as a false joy and peace, the Christian must wait to discover where the inspiration leads. Does it lead to humility or to pride, to self-forgetfulness or self-centeredness?

There is a kind of sadness for instance, when one is sharing in Christ's passion. But this sadness will also be peaceful if it genuinely shares in the suffering of Christ's mystical body. We call this type of sadness «compassion.» We know whether the experience is from the good or evil spirit by the end-product: «by their fruits shall you know them.» Does it take the person out of himself or not? Sadness can be the touch of the Savior purifying a man or the impulse of Satan tempting him to sin. It may lead him to a progressive understanding of the things of God and eventually to joy or deeper consolation, or it may lead him to discouragement, to frantic pleasure-seeking, or to bitterness.

Now, we often hear the remark, «Father, I've made my decision and I'm really at peace.» But the peace he has attained may not come from the good spirit. It may be only the natural release of tension that accompanies a decision. Often such a person has not considered all the evidence and is working with subjective criteria alone. He has yet to con-

196

sider the objective criteria of discernment.

The first objective criterion is charity: «Be ambitious for the higher gifts. And I am going to show you a way that is better than any of them. If I have all the eloquence of men or of angels, but speak without love, I am simply a gong booming or a cymbal clashing.» (1 Co 12:31; 13:1) St. Paul goes on to point out that this criterion of love surpasses the subjective experience of talking in tongues and the other charismatic gifts.

The second criterion is the willingness to follow Christ through all the events of his gospel, especially the passion. The third criterion is subordination to the Holy Spirit, operating within our holy Mother, the hierarchical church. In other words, we must be docile to the Spirit as he speaks to us through other persons, through the community, through legitimate authority. Thus, the process of subjective discernment must be balanced by a consideration of these objective criteria.

There are people who have received one or another of the various charismatic gifts, such as the gift of tongues. How do you treat such a person? The same as others. How has the gift affected him? Has it become a form of «riches» to him? How does he behave in community? Is he more relaxed, more free? Is he more generous, more loving? Does he show the other exterior signs of the good spirit? Or has he become critical and exclusive?

When giving spiritual direction, you soon discover that only the person under direction can make the discernment. If the exercitant is open and if he tells you everything, then you can serve as an objective norm. You can help him to see whether he is being deceived or not and help to spot where the movement is leading him. But he is the only one that really knows whether there is an uplift of soul or not. He has to tell you how he is being moved.

What is happening to you as a director is also important in the discerning process. As director you are somehow a resonator of what is going on in your client. And, yet, it is only if the client speaks and explains to you what is happening that you can become this resonator. It is then necessary to discern in yourself some of the affective movements in your own being, or you will not be the objective norm best able to help your client discern.

In some instances special gifts (even charismatic gifts) can lead to cliquishness. A sign of the good spirit is a willingness to live with all kinds of persons. Sometimes you can check this willingness by your client's reaction to obedience. Thus, the objective signs of charity and of obedience to the church and to the community enable you to verify the subjective experience of the person. Such norms will help to determine whether the person is being deluded.

The next two rules throw further light on the puzzling reactions that occur within your client. With their aid he can learn to recognize patterns in himself and anticipate the movements of the evil spirit:

> We must carefully observe the whole course of our thoughts. If the beginning and middle and end of the course of thoughts are wholly good and directed to what is entirely right, it is a sign that they are from the good angel. But the course of thoughts suggested to us may terminate in something evil, or distracting, or less good... or by destroying the peace, tranquillity, and quiet which it had before, it may cause disturbance to the soul. These things are a clear sign that the thoughts are proceeding from the evil spirit. [333]

> When the enemy of our human nature has been

detected and recognized by the trail of evil marking his course and by the wicked end to which he leads us, it will be profitable for one who has been tempted to review immediately the whole course of the temptation. Let him consider the series of good thoughts, how they arose, how the evil one gradually attempted to make him step down from the state of spiritual delight and joy in which he was, till finally he drew him to his wicked designs. The purpose of this review is that once such an experience has been understood and carefully observed, we may guard ourselves for the future against the customary deceits of the enemy. [334]

These rules also afford a fuller understanding of the examination of conscience. In an effort to use the examen to greater advantage, one can ask: «How did this experience start? What's to be done about it?» Or, if he experiences peace and consolation and joy, he asks: «Where did this peace come from?» Such an examination of conscience conforms to the rules of the «Second Week»; it can help to anticipate movements and attitudes of soul. Through such an examination of conscience, a man can level off the ups and downs of consolation and desolation.

In the colloquies of the «Third Exercise» of the «First Week,» the retreatant asks for a more profound self-knowledge. While these rules of the «Second Week» apply to generous souls, a man is not always constant in his generosity. One function of the daily examination of conscience, therefore, is to renew the purification originally achieved in the «First Week,» and another is the sort of detachment more characteristic of the «Second Week.» In fact, the whole pattern of the Exercises is repeated in the daily examination of conscience.

The seventh rule reminds us of our Lord's parable about

the man who sweeps one devil out of his house only to have it taken over by seven others. (*cf.* Lk 11:24-26)

> In souls that are progressing to greater perfection, the action of the good angel is delicate, gentle, delightful. ... The action of the evil spirit upon such souls is violent, noisy, and disturbing. ... When the disposition is contrary to that of the spirits, they enter with noise and commotion that are easily perceived. When the disposition is similar to that of the spirits, they enter silently, as one coming into his own house when the doors are open. [335]

With this seventh rule the question of peace arises. «Is there peace? Is it a true peace or a false peace?» One sign that the peace comes from the good spirit is the person's obedience and docility. Sometimes in a thirty-day retreat the director may wish to see whether the person is obedient or docile. Charmot has an article in *Finding God in All Things* [16] on the criteria for distinguishing good and evil spirits. In it he speaks about the different stages through which a person passes when he is being guided by the good spirit.

The first stage is confusion. It is not so much the ordinary confusion of everyday life, but the confusion in the face of special graces. He cannot understand why he should be given this grace, this vision, this project, this apostolate. Why is the Lord choosing him? He feels he has none of the talents required for this kind of vocation. Like St. Peter when called by Christ, he feels impelled to say: «Leave me, Lord; I am a sinful man.» (Lk 5:8)

The second stage is detachment. He is free interiorly with the experience which he thinks may be a call. If the spiritual director tells him he cannot follow such a call and he reacts peacefully, then he has a sense of indifference; he is ready for anything that God asks.

200

The third stage is profound peace with the Holy Spirit. The fourth is obedience with an unselfish heart. When the person gives himself to his neighbor, there is growth in generosity, a growth in service, and a growth in devotion to others. At the same time, he grows more and more in the desire and need for the interior life. The signs of the evil spirit's operation, as described by Charmot, indicate contrary reactions: vanity, pride, disquiet, stubbornness, self-will, rebellion, discouragement, inactivity, and (eventually) serious sin.

Someone might ask whether a person who is not obedient to the Hierarchical Church could be at peace with the Holy Spirit. In certain circumstances an individual might decide to leave the Church, and yet he might experience peace in doing so. But because he sees the Church only as a structured thing, it is bound to be only a temporary peace. Since the Church actually is the concrete extension of Christ, this opting out sometimes shows the person that the true problem is rooted in himself. He carries himself with him wherever he goes. Then in his humility he may gain a deeper understanding of the Church, an acceptance of her human weaknesses and a more correct form of obedience.

But the movement of the Spirit is always towards Christ and his Church and so to the Father. An atheist who is at peace in his atheism will be moved towards Christ usually through his contact with other Christians. Gradually he may come to see the possibility of Christianity. Often however, the atheist has no contact with true Christians. He never actually experiences the Church in her goodness.

The Catholic who opts out is in a different situation. Normally this choice would be due, not to a movement of the Spirit, but to a lack of true Catholic witness. Yet this man may be rejecting a false image of the Church, and thereby he may be finding peace. The root of such discontent is often just such a false image of the Church. A man may picture the Church as a social-work organization only; if so, his concept of the Church is incomplete. The Church should be interested in social work, but that does not form the totality of the Church's mission. So in opting out the Christian may not be leaving the real Church but demanding that she be what she is not.

Father Daniel Berrigan once said that a man cannot be a prophet outside the Church; prophecy occurs only within the Church. I believe this to be true. Moreover, a prophet had better be willing to suffer within the Church. True prophecy involves suffering in peace. Some may be called to purify the Church as prophets, then they will have to stay with her through thick and thin.

A person may leave in good faith; no one should pronounce judgment on him. If his good faith endures, the Spirit will lead him to Christ in one way or another. But to find Christ always means to find the Church. What is needed with this kind of person is lots of patience, lots of endurance, and lots of discernment. Probably what is needed most is lots of love — a love rooted in one's own faith that the individual in question is loved by God.

The eighth rule, like the second one, speaks of «consolation without previous cause.» This is an experience that the person alone can judge. It is self-authenticating and becomes very important in determining a vocation (as will be seen in the next chapter). But it is in the period following this consolation that «the soul frequently forms various resolutions and plans which are not granted directly by God our Lord.» [336] These words of Ignatius are important for the whole discussion on vocations.

For a religious to consider leaving his community is, of course, quite different from his leaving the Church. In the discerning process it is important to know whether the person originally experienced the call from God in a state of freedom. Such a call might be called a «core experience.» It is one in which a person is aware in the totality of his being that he is being called permanently to this religious family.

The person may feel peace in his decision to leave religious life. Now, just as with the person leaving the Church, this peace may be false, but one cannot be as sure about its falsity. The peace he is relying on for discernment may be false, but it may also be true. If it is true then usually it becomes apparent that he did not have a vocation in the first place. His reasons for joining the religious community may have been extremely mixed. Even the popular image of the Church in his locality may have influenced him wrongly. Moreover, all kinds of false reasons could have kept him in the community for many years. At this juncture it is quite possible that the Spirit is asking him to leave.

Perhaps he should go back and review again his motives for entering. Why did he make the decision to enter in the first place? His original decision may have rested on false or irrelevant reasons. He may realize now that he belonged to a group in his class for whom vows were a kind of graduation ceremony. He may have taken vows to gain status. His mother and father may have over-influenced his decision. Or he may have simply felt at home with certain kind religious friends or teachers.Thus, he recalls and tries to discern the original experience. Then he may see, with the help of a director, that there were no signs of a genuine call. In the light of that insight the trend of his last five or six years only verifies the fact that he had no vocation in the first place.

Nor is a mere willingness to suffer the sole criterion of a vocation. There are other criteria, such as generosity, openness of soul, charity. The individual may be saying to himself, «Since I have to suffer with Christ, I'll find peace in suffering.» Well and good, so far as it goes, but if he ends by turning in on himself so that there is no magnanimity of soul, no moving out from this suffering, no growth in generosity, then his peace is false.

I remember a novice I was directing two or three years ago who was having a difficult time. We went through the Exercises together, and in the «Third Week» he seemed to come to what I thought was true peace, the ability to accept the burdens of religious life in peace. His new attitude was connected with the crucifixion and passion, and he seemed for the moment to be making a good decision. About a month later, however, he dropped back into the kind of sadness, anxiety and social difficulties that he had experienced before making the Exercises.

So I discussed this turn of events with him. He agreed that, to be a Christian, a man must be willing to take up his cross and follow Christ. He was willing, he said, to take up that cross; he could see the need for it in his life. But he seemed to stop there, preoccupied with himself and rather depressed. Meanwhile, he had become a serious trial to the rest of the community. His continued lack of response in that area led me to conclude that he had no real vocation.

Joy in suffering is a very difficult thing to express. It is not merely resignation in suffering. There has to be an expansiveness of heart, an expansiveness of soul, that is present as well. It is not endurance alone but a conviction that this suffering is what the Lord wants. And there is a kind of joy in the humiliation of not being a good sufferer. If there is no joy in the trials of religious life, then the usual practice in discerning is to go back to the first decision.

An individual may lack peace in religious life because he has no vocation, or because he is still working through the problems of human maturity and early religious growth. But it may also be the sign of a new spiritual demand on the person, an urging towards fuller abandonment to the person of Jesus. The person may be experiencing a variety of the «dark night of the senses.» Then his need is to discern, not a true vocation, but rather the direction in which the Spirit is leading him in this state of life.

Another false discernment arises when a person says he is certain of that first decision, certain that God was calling him to religious life, and this seems to be correct. But now he thinks God is calling him to be married. Then he begins theorizing about «the God of process» and about «the phenomenon of constant change in this world of ours.» Eventually he questions the reality of commitments themselves. He is in need of prayer and reflection on permanent commitment.

The permanent commitment of the marriage vows is to the point here. Both persons are changing, and yet each is committed to the other. The commitment is person to person. It is not a commitment to this woman insofar as she has a good figure, nor to this man insofar as he remains young and handsome. It is a commitment of John to Jane, of Jane to John, who are persons throughout their lives. This is the reason why human beings can make a permanent commitment: their interpersonal exchange finds its source in the fidelity of the divine Persons.

Commitment in a religious community has the same source of fidelity and permanence. The religious does not commit himself to a set of constitutions, nor to a way of life, nor to the apostolate, but to persons, primarily to the person of Christ. After this commitment to Christ, all the other things follow: constitutions, way of life, apostolate, and so on.

Intention is an important part of commitment, both in religious life and in marriage. Even though a couple has gone through the sacramental ceremony of marriage, there may not be this commitment of person to person. If so, there is no marriage, but this is very difficult to determine from external evidence. Similarly, one may externally pronounce the solemn vows of profession, but the personal gift of self to God may be withheld.

Intention is important for another reason. Many religious have committed themselves to an apostolate or to a group of persons but have not really committed themselves to the spirit of that group. In my own order, for example, the Jesuit somehow commits himself to the spirit of Ignatius, and he identifies himself with Ignatius. The Franciscan does the same thing with regard to St. Francis, and the Dominican and the Benedictine to their respective founders. When I meet a Jesuit who does not understand Ignatius or who does not cherish the ideals of Ignatius or cannot grasp the Ignatian spirit, I wonder whether he is a Jesuit. A further aspect of my personal commitment to Christ in the religious state is expressed through commitment to Ignatius and his companions down the centuries. The spirit of each founder is significant for all members.

Again, the call to celibacy or to poverty is distinct, not only from the call to marriage, but from the call to a religious community as well. A person may be called to private vows and not to public vows with a group. This latter vocation is often more difficult to discern. Thus, there is good reason for the long period usually required before final vows. It seems to follow that if a person in a religious community begins to question his vocation, he still has to discern the separate matter of private vows.

It is important to distinguish one's vocation from one's state of life. In the *Exercises* Ignatius considers a mistaken but «unchangeable choice» of life. His view is that a person must remain in his state of life even though he may have entered it

206

without a divine call: «Since such a choice was inordinate and awry, it does not seem to be a vocation from God, as many erroneously believe. They make a divine call out of a perverse and wicked choice. For every vocation that comes from God is always pure and undefiled, uninfluenced by the flesh or any inordinate attachment.» [172] We must remember, of course, the grave abuses of his day, to which he is no doubt alluding here.

The practice of the Church has changed since the time of Ignatius. Actually, in context, he speaks only about marriage and the priesthood; he does not mention religious vocations. Today, if people cannot at all find peace and contentment in the religious community, the Church is more ready to dismiss and dispense from vows. Nevertheless, it is possible that this does not completely resolve the question of vocation.

A vocation is not a static thing. The original person-to-person call becomes known at a certain point in time with great clarity and authenticity. This time is always important for discernment. But the vocation itself is an ongoing relationship between the person and Christ. What happens later may call into question an earlier discernment, or it may indicate that one is moving away from his vocation and sinning. In this case the person should pray to stir up the grace that is within him, as Paul says to Timothy. (2 Tm 1:6)

A vocation is a free gift; one may reject it initially without sinning. Still, after a person has made a public commitment through vows and has accepted his vocation, if he subsequently leaves through his own fault, sin may be involved. It is possible for a person to lose his vocation, that is, the dynamic giving of himself to Christ in religious life, through a series of faults, not always his own, but in many instances those of the community. He may have lost his vitality, his desire, his magnanimity of soul. Even the great call of Christ to be an apostle no longer

207

appeals to him. His whole commitment to Christ gradually diminishes and he sinks into a lifeless state as far as being a religious is concerned. But it is his fault, or at least there is some human fault along the way. What usually happens is that such a person does not want to discern again. If he recognizes and repents his sin, the Lord forgives him and he begins a new way of life.

In confronting the question of vocation, a religious may need to discern a number of times before he can achieve a new identification with the spirit of the founder. Thus, there may be a number of core experiences in the process. In the discerning of a vocation the person uses this kind of experience as a norm against which to judge the experience that he is now undergoing. This non-conceptual experience of God which Ignatius refers to [330, 336] becomes the criterion of whether the consolations that verify his call are of the same order.

In this discussion on the rules of discernment of the «Second Week,» it has become apparent that the spiritual life does not cease to develop even after the conversion experience of the «First Week.» Man is always growing, constantly finding himself and God through his relations with Jesus Christ and with his fellow men. The movements of his own self-centered security as well as the grandiose suggestions of the evil one constantly combine in an effort to deceive him and lead him into a false security or misguided orientation of his life.

Possibly one of the main signs of the good spirit's action is the call to insecurity — that is, to a life of total dependency on God. That is why he needs spiritual direction and must pray for deep humility. When a person learns to suspect his own motives, he will seek out the spiritual guidance of one who is sent by the Lord. (Jn 17:18; 20:21) Then he will be aware that discernment takes place in the name of Jesus, and he can rest in the words of Christ: «where two or three meet in my name, I shall be there with them.» (Mt 18:20)

CHAPTER 13

CHOOSING A STATE OF LIFE

It is not every spirit, my dear people, that you can trust; test them, to see if they come from God, there are many false prophets, now, in the world. You can tell the spirits that come from God by this: every spirit which acknowledges that Jesus the Christ has come in the flesh is from God; but any spirit which will not say this of Jesus is not from God, but is the spirit of Antichrist, whose coming you were warned about. Well, now he is here, in the world. Children, you have already overcome these false prophets, because you are from God and you have in you one who is greater than anyone in this world; as for them, they are of the world, and so they speak the language of the world and the world listens to them. But we are children of God, and those who know God listen to us; those who are not of God refuse to listen to us. This is how we can tell the spirit of truth from the spirit of falsehood. (1 Jn 4:1-6)

Here is how Ignatius introduces his method for choosing a state of life:

Many first choose marriage, which is a means, and secondarily the service of God our Lord in marriage, though the service of God is the end. So also others first choose to have benefices, and afterwards to serve God in them. Such persons do not go directly to God,

> but want God to conform wholly to their inordinate attachments. Consequently, they make of the end a means, and of the means an end. As a result, what they ought to seek first, they seek last. [169]

This often happens with religious. Many men and women enter religious life for the wrong reasons. The hope is that, when they have been in the community for a while, the proper motive will arise, at least before final vows, and preferably before first vows. The point Ignatius is making is that each individual's first aim should be to serve God, which is the end, and then to seek the means of doing this in a particular state of life. Nothing must move him to use such means or to deprive himself of them save only the service and praise of God our Lord and the salvation of his soul. The same principle should be used by people who wish to change their state of life.

Ignatius considers matters about which a choice may be made. [170-174] He speaks about «unchangeable choices,» such as priesthood and marriage. What he says in the third point [172] implies that a person can be in the priesthood, religious life, or marriage without a divine vocation. He mentions a choice that has been inordinate and awry, and he argues that «it does not seem to be a vocation from God, as many erroneously believe. ... For every vocation that comes from God is always pure and undefiled, uninfluenced by the flesh or any inordinate attachment.» [172]

Whether the person can pinpoint some core experience or religious experience at the beginning is not as important as his present awareness that he has a call from the Lord. But if a person does not feel that he has had a call from the Lord at any time in his religious life, he does not necessarily have a divine vocation even though he is living in a religious community. At one time there was a fairly widespread conviction that if you lived long enough in a religious community, you had a divine vocation. It does not follow. Thus, we must be open to the need for discerning whether or not a religious has a vocation from God.

The Exercises are basically designed to help a man or woman find the Lord's will in choosing a state of life. But they can be useful as well for confirmation of a choice. Ignatius indicates three times when a correct and good choice of life may be made in the context of faith. The first is when God so moves the soul that there can be no mistaking his call. He instances the calls of Matthew and of Paul. Many more people than we imagine have such self-authenticating experiences. I will return to this later.

If a person has not had a religious experience analogous to that of the apostles, then Ignatius gives two other times for determining one's state of life. The second time is «When much light and understanding are derived through experience of desolations and consolations and discernment of diverse spirits.» [176] In the midst of desolations and consolations the retreatant is free and generous. He wants to do the will of God, but he is being moved this way and that. He is being exercised over his decision. It is by discerning the movement of spirits that he discovers whether he has a vocation or not.

The third time is a «time of tranquility.» One considers first for what purpose man is born, that is, for the praise of God our Lord and for the salvation of his soul.» [177] This third time is one of peace and calm. The person is in a flat calm: no storms, not even any breezes disturb his tranquility. For such a time Ignatius supplies further suggestions. It is important to remember that it is «a time when the soul is not agitated by

212

different spirits, and has free and peaceful use of its natural powers.» [177]

Ignatius outlines «two ways» of discovering what the Lord wants from a person. The first of these ways can look very rationalistic, a businesslike weighing of the *pros* and *cons* regarding marriage with the *pros* and *cons* of the religious life. If there are a hundred *pros* for marriage and only three *cons,* and on the other hand only ten for the religious life and sixty against it, then the person may think the Lord wants him to be married. But this is not exactly what Ignatius says. One is first to hold oneself in freedom «like a balance at equilibrium,» [179] and then he is to weigh the motives, not merely count the *pros* and *cons*. One *pro* may outweigh all of the *cons,* and vice-versa.

But this is not the end of the process. For, after all this reasoning, the person still has to go to God in prayer in order to seek confirmation. In the sixth point Ignatius says: «After such a choice or decision, the one who has made it must turn with great diligence to prayer in the presence of God our Lord, and offer Him his choice that the Divine Majesty may deign to accept and confirm it if it is for His greater service and praise.» [183] How is he going to know whether the divine Majesty accepts and confirms his decision? Not from what he has gone through in his reasoning process, but from some affective experience of consolation.

When describing the second way of choosing, Ignatius suggests the techniques of role playing, imagining oneself giving advice, or placing oneself on his deathbed. [186, 187] Similarly, a person can be asked to imagine his life in a certain state with its joys and sufferings. For example, one might imagine the hardship and sufferings that would be entailed if he should go as a missionary to Africa. Are the imaginings romantic or realistic? Does he dream of himself as another St. John Brebeuf dying for Christ in torment? Or does he see the ignorance of the people, their poverty, their hostility, the difficulty in trying to teach them?

The advice given at the end of the «first way» [183] also concludes the three considerations of the «second way.» [184-187] No real confirmation of vocation can be gained from the reasoning process by itself. These first and second ways often become the occasion for some kind of affective movement. There has to be an affective response in the person before the judgment can be made. In fact, many religious agree that at one time or another they have had the affective confirmation of their vocation.

This need for confirmation takes us back to the second time, «When much light and understanding are derived through experience of desolations and consolations and discernment of diverse spirits.» [176] As Karl Rahner notes in his *Dynamic Element in the Church* [10] this confirmation is sought in accord with the second and eighth rules for discernment in the «Second Week.»

As I have noted already, the director's role in this situation is to be an objective norm for the exercitant who is trying to determine the will of God for himself. The director's job is to help the person find peace and freedom with the Holy Spirit. This means that the director himself must also be free and at peace. For example, many people make retreats in order to determine whether or not they should leave their religious community. But others are fearful and unwilling to face the Spirit before making a decision to leave. Because the director needs to be a rock of strength on such occasions, he cannot allow himself to become excessively elated or disturbed, but he must steadily guide his client towards a deeper level of discernment.

One day a religious of many years said to me during his

214

retreat: «Jesus is truly a wonderful person! I had never met him before.» This man had finally attained dispositions which enabled him to make a real decision with respect to his vocation. He had originally entered because two or three good friends of his in school were entering at the time. He stayed for the same reasons. But, as final vows and ordination approached, he realized that he had to decide independently. He made a retreat and, as a result, he eventually left the order. Many other persons have done the same thing, persons who are truly concerned about serving the Lord. Stay or leave, they know their decision has to flow from freedom.

Now, you may feel that a person you are guiding in retreat made a right decision some six or seven years earlier — because you knew him then. Maybe you were in charge of the novitiate when he made vows. But now he feels he should leave the order. What is your attitude to be? Outside retreat, you can use all the arguments available; in retreat he must be left free. He must freely decide to stay or leave. And as director you have to make an act of faith that, if this is his vocation, the Lord will make it known to him.

Ignatius points out that counsel given outside the Exercises differs in certain respects from counseling during the Exercises. Outside the retreat, he says, we may «lawfully and meritoriously» urge those who have the right qualifications to go to the sacraments, form habits of mental prayer, take vows, and advance to «every form of religious perfection.» [15] But during the Spiritual Exercises the Lord himself should be allowed to speak to the heart of the retreatant. Ignatius even adds that the director should not seek to learn the private thoughts or sins of the exercitant, but should concentrate instead on the movement of various spirits that may occur in him. [17] The director must not urge him to take vows, to leave or to remain in religious

215

life, or to any other decision. If you do not feel that you can be this free with a given retreatant or he with you, then someone else should direct him.

The question will arise, «Since he has made perpetual vows, is he free to consider another decision?» One's first reaction is «No; he has made his decision. All he can do is to learn to live with his commitment.» But then another question occurs: «What about his life of free service? Has he lost this freedom?» Religious commitment should certainly lead to greater freedom. If one is going to continue in a religious community, then he should continue with more freedom and more conviction. It follows that the person must be given the freedom to decide at this moment that he should continue to accept his religious vows. Vows should increase, not decrease, a person's freedom, and the director must have faith and trust in that freedom. He has to believe that a true vocation will surface again.

But a man needs to be in a position where there is a real possibility for it to surface again. For example, at the time that he is trying to determine whether he has a vocation to the religious life, he cannot be on the point of marrying a woman whom he loves. Since his involvement with her simply removes the possibility of freedom, he cannot (without self-deception) make a real discernment at that time. Usually an extended retreat situation is needed if the Spirit is to operate within him.

When he is re-examining his vocation, it is essential for him to be brought again into a position of freedom. In that freedom he has to consider the possibility that he did not have a vocation seven or so years before, and he has to be in the position to confirm the vocation. And unless you, as a spiritual director, allow that kind of freedom, he may not receive any confirmation at all.

Even a person who feels called to a religious vocation and is simultaneously acting against his call, ought to be left free.

What do I mean by that? I mean that the director must have faith in the Holy Spirit. If the individual is truly called, the strength of the Spirit will win through and prove it. If he does not have a vocation, he should not enter religious life anyway. Of course, the man who is rethinking his vocation is in a somewhat different position. He may have made at least an external commitment seven years before; he did so in good faith and after considerable prayer and direction. In the process of discernment, therefore, he must take that first experience with complete seriousness.

When the exercitant is considering the different states of life, it may be necessary for the director to correct some misconceptions on perfection. Marriage is a valid vocation and a way of sanctity. At one time many felt that if one wanted to be perfect and follow the Lord, he had to enter a religious community. But Vatican II has made it very clear that there is no state of life that is subjectively more perfect than another. Objectively, the evangelical state of life may be better than any other state of life. But as far as the individual is concerned, no state of life is better than any other. The best state of life for an individual is the one to which the Lord is calling him.

Once the exercitant feels he knows his vocation, a good exercise is to pray as if he were on his deathbed. There should be a sense of fulfillment on his deathbed because he was married and had brought forth several children, or an experience of fulfillment on his deathbed because he was a religious and had brought the word of God to people, consoled them and led them to the resurrected Christ.

A religious call may begin with an experience of crisis or temptation, but full recognition of that call can be affirmed only when the person has reached tranquility, a sense of wholeness, of integration, peace and humility. Then he will recognize that the totality of his being will find its meaning only in this way of life.

Disorder and lack of peace are signs that the time of election has not arrived. More investigation is needed, more acceptance of self, more prayer and penance, until there is peace with oneself, with God and with whatever God reveals and wishes. But this is also the time when the devil may act as an angel of light. The final decision should be confirmed by an abiding peace in the person so that he can say, «This fits me; this is who I am.» Of course, other confirming signs are the objective criteria, such as the abiding peace which an individual enjoys in the community and the Church.

Concerning the experience undergone in determining vocations, Abraham Maslow has written a pamphlet entitled, *Religions, Values, and Peak Experiences.*[5] Research on this topic included a survey of peak experiences. When he began his project he was convinced that few people had peak experiences. But he discovered just the opposite: practically everyone in the survey had had a peak experience at one time or another. Even those who said they had not had peak experiences, he discovered, were hiding them for some reason.

A deep experience of the action of God upon a person can become the criterion for judging his other religious experiences and his choice of a state of life. Over and above these subjective experiences, there are the objective criteria of the Church. One example in the religious life is the long test of stability before final vows.

Besides the core experiences which can be quite undifferentiated in a younger person, later in life there can be experiences of identification. As a person realizes his own identity, he is able to integrate his earlier experiences. He may have such a strong awareness of Christ's call that he cannot doubt its reality. It is not just an emotional or overly sentimental experience. It is an experience in the depth of his being, and he knows it. He has to discern it, of course, but it is there. In fact, a person may have a number of these core experiences or religious experiences independently of the vocation call.

People do experience the action of God. They can have crises of faith, hope and charity in the everyday living of the Christian life. And in some of these crises the Lord lifts the person out of himself. He experiences the grace which takes him beyond himself.

The Lord's way of responding to man's crisis may possibly account for the present phenomenon of pentecostalism. In recent years great numbers of people have been experiencing a lack of faith and have come close to despair. Hence they have tried various and somewhat bizarre methods to gain fulfillment and meaning. At this juncture the Lord may give special signs to indicate his abiding presence and love. Obviously these extraordinary experiences of God's activity must be carefully examined in accord with the rules of the «Second Week.»

God's consolation may be either mediated or immediate. When consolation is mediated, it comes through a created being, another person, the liturgy, Scripture, the beauties of nature, or any incidental event. Even though mediated, it remains God's consolation and an expression of his love.

In addition, God consoles the soul by his immediate presence «without any previous cause.» [330] This is an experience involving the presence of God alone. It cannot be anticipated or recalled. It would seem to be a non-conceptual awareness of presence.

God can enter or leave the soul when he wants. Ignatius says, «there can be no deception in it, since it can proceed from God our Lord only.» [336] The experience validates itself beyond possibility of description or reproduction. It is a «given»; what is «given» is an experience of the Lord's gift of himself. In a letter to Sister Teresa Rejadella, Ignatius describes this experience in these words: «That is to say, he [God] begins to speak within us without any sound of words, he draws up the soul wholly to his love and gives us a sense of himself, so that even if we wished, we could not resist. This interior feeling ... is filled with deep humility, for, of course, it is God's own Spirit that governs in everything [17].»

That experience then becomes the touchstone for all his other experiences of consolation. Since only the individual himself has this experience, he alone can compare it with his experiences. He alone can judge whether other experiences are valid and determine their meaning.

This may even apply to the matter of vocation. The experience of vocation needs to be compared with a previous or subsequent experience of God's action for the person needs other experiences of desolation and consolation in order to judge ongoing experiences. The director, of course, can be of assistance here in helping the person recognize the quality of his experience.

It is possible that a person could have the experience of consolation without previous cause at the time that he is making his election. Such an experience could possibly be a confirmation of the call, but not necessarily. One should be cautious at this time because in the afterglow of consolation the desire to commit himself may not be for his good or for God's glory. For it is in the afterglow that one can be led by the evil spirit disguised as an angel of light. [cf. 336]

When Ignatius talks about consolation without previous cause, he is not necessarily speaking about a call. But a call may be supported by such an experience. The confirmation of the

220

call may require a long time. If the conviction that one has a vocation persists through severe testing and suffering, then there is good objective reason for trusting that call. The person himself may say to you, «I never doubted the call.»

All three «times» are often experienced by the same person. He may have a very strong conviction that God is calling him, but this conviction needs further discernment. He may go through a second time in which he finds himself free, and yet experiences many sorts of spiritual movements. Or again, he may find himself in peace but in ignorance of what the Lord wants.

When choosing a state of life, exceptional freedom is needed so that God may reveal his will to the retreatant. In chapters 1 and 3 we considered the primary freedom that a person must achieve if he is to make a decision about the ultimate meaning of his life: with God's grace he must liberate himself from inordinate attachments. But even in matters of secondary significance, such as one's life style or the choice of a state of life, an unusually high degree of freedom will be required.

Perhaps this kind of freedom may last only until the end of the Exercises, but the retreatant will be aware of it while he has it and will be able to recognize the operation of the Spirit. Such an awareness will give him assurance of a right decision. Often when one leaves the Exercises, he drops back into unfreedom. But there is a difference: he knows that he made his decision in a state of freedom. Moreover, he knows his weaknesses and his limitations, and he knows what he has to pray for. He sees himself differently and he understands how God operates in his life. From his new found awareness of himself and his experience of consolations and desolations he can begin to «find God in all things.»

In a source outside the *Exercises,* Ignatius presents a *schema* of progressively alternating choices by which one is moved to election. Typically it concerns the question of vocation. The retreatant first poses the choice between marriage and the single life: «I propose, if it be your will, to get married.» After a pause long enough to notice any interior reaction and to discern its nature, he proposes the alternative: «I propose, if it be your will, to live a single life.»

If there should be a clear interior reaction one way or the other, the retreatant continues with proposals which progressively specify the form of the Christian life God indicates as fulfilling his design. He considers the possibilities in the single state. Is he to live as a single person in the world, or as a person with vows? Is he to live as a person with public vows or as a person with private vows? If he is to be a person with public vows, the next step is to try to determine what kind of religious congregation, and so forth. In this method the Spirit is given room to operate and to bring a sense of fulfillment and well-being, a sense of harmony with the one state rather than the other. In some instances the harmony is accompanied by experiences of great consolation.

The choice of a state of life affords the clearest instance of an «either-or» situation. But the same method can be used in making any significant decision. If one can be free from inordinate attachments, then there can be various movements of the spirits. When a man has achieved that freedom, a certain harmony develops between the Spirit and himself. Then the good spirit will give consolation as a sign for one or the other side of an «either-or» decision. Ignatius suggests that the retreatant divide his problem into an «either-or» scheme and then ask in prayer: «Should I do this?» or «Shouldn't I?» In this way the problem moves towards a «yes-no» solution, and the answer is provided in terms of consolation. [cf. 178-183]

In the second time of election, when there is a movement

of spirits, the crucial question is whether the movement comes from the good or evil spirit. Why is that? Because in a time of consolation it is the good spirit who inspires the man at prayer. In his «Rules of the First Week» Ignatius notes explicitly: «just as in consolation the good spirit guides and counsels us, so in desolation the evil spirit guides and counsels.» [318]

How can you know if the person you are directing has a vocation and whether the consolation he receives is from God? Only if he confirms it with a consolation he does not doubt, [336] or by testing the consolation against the suffering normally entailed in a certain state of life. In this process, you are hoping that the Lord will give him consolation as a sign that one state is preferable to another. Now, over a period of four or five days, or even a longer period, Ignatius expects some kind of consolation or desolation to take place. If there is nothing happening, the director may suggest some penance or extra time of prayer. [cf. 6,17]

Let us take the example of a person who is considering a choice between the married state and the religious life. If the choice is to be made in the second time, there will be some movement of soul, experiences of fear, perhaps, or of joy, experiences of separation from the Lord or closeness to the Lord. And in the contemplations of the public life, the person may feel very strongly the call of Christ.

The director tries to analyze the experience objectively. For example, the retreatant tells him that in his prayer he experienced consolation when he thought about marriage. In response to questioning, he starts to describe the woman he loves, her personality, her character, all that attracts him to her. Well, if you are the director, you begin to wonder how much is egotistical and how much is unselfish. Then you may say to him, «That's fine. Consider yourself a married man with four children, living in a house with a heavy mortgage, while there's trouble at the plant. Imagine coming home and finding that your wife hasn't cleaned up the house (it is a real mess), hasn't prepared your dinner yet and is chatting away on the phone.» Ask him to pray over this situation, to pray on the difficulties and suffering of the married state, and to relate these to the life of Christ.

Similarly with the person who feels called to be a religious. He describes his prayer on the mountain top, with a predieu beautifully padded and covered in fine velvet, a gilded prayer book and an exquisite ivory crucifix. And he feels he has been raised to the seventh heaven with St. Paul. Once again, you present him with the difficulties of the religious life. For example, ask him to imagine himself suffering trials of obedience in a specific case. Does the consolation continue when he considers these negative factors? Is there a joy in suffering for Christ such as is desired in the third kind of humility? It is important to know the movement of spirits that occurs when the person thinks of the difficulties that belong to the vocation and state of life he is thinking about.

Concerning this technique of using consolations and desolations to discern a vocation, Ignatius says that it is more important for the director to know the interior movements of the exercitant than his private thoughts. [17] Thus, he should ask questions of this nature. «How did you feel? Were you joyful? Did you feel sorry? Did the prayer go quickly or did it go slowly? Did you sense that you were in the presence of God? Was God absent to you?»

Sometimes the director may ask, «Was the Scripture text really meaningful to you? In what way?» The director does not want a detailed description of the thoughts that went on in the person's mind during meditation, nor a list of his insights.

He is more interested in how the exercitant felt. Those feelings are the expression of consolation or desolation. [*cf.* 316, 317] These consolations and desolations can then be judged by comparing them with a previous consolation that you know is not deceptive. This, of course, is the result of much self-awareness, much reflecting on those experiences of harmony and peace in one's being that give one the ability to judge oneself in relation to God and his action on the inner self.

Ignatius suggests specific mysteries in the public life of our Lord for contemplation during these six or seven days. Those he indicates seem to have been chosen with a view to the decision on a state of life. They are not necessarily important for other kinds of decision. In other words, I think that the director might select other mysteries to meet a particular need of the exercitant. He may feel strongly that someone should be contemplating the woman washing our Lord's feet, or the woman at the well, or Nicodemus. But I think that Ignatius has chosen this particular set of mysteries because he views the Exercises as an instrument for deciding one's state of life. These contemplations are well adapted for that subject.

Notice that the contemplations of the public life follow the same pattern as the contemplations on the «Incarnation» and on the «Nativity,» except that the «Triple Colloquy» is recommended, as is the note at the end of the «Three Classes of Men.» It is interesting that Ignatius now assigns only one contemplation a day, whereas in the «Hidden Life» he assigned two. I think the reason is that, if a person is trying to make a decision about a state of life, then that decision is going to lurk in his mind throughout the day. Accordingly, Ignatius simplifies the prayer; he reduces the matter to one contemplation and recommends the method of repetition. [62, 118, 119, 159]

For the fifth day he selects «The contemplation on the

journey of Christ our Lord from Nazareth to the River Jordan and His baptism.» [158] There is not very much in the way of material — only about four verses in Matthew's gospel. Many people can make several contemplations on our Lord's leaving home, even on the one phrase, «he came from Galilee.»(Mt 3:13)

This contemplation is the beginning of a decision-making process for Christ. He «leaves father, mother, brother, and sister»; he leaves his mother for the Father's sake. He leaves his homeland, Nazareth. He becomes a wandering Aramean like his ancestor Abraham. Since it is a time of decision as he proceeds down the Jordan valley he might be recalling the history of Israel and its confrontation with Yahweh. We see the Spirit working in Christ — first descending upon him at his baptism, and then driving him off into the desert. Especially at this moment, the Spirit is drawing Jesus to the Father.

It is the Holy Spirit who leads him to accept baptism, the same Holy Spirit who is praying in us. Jesus is baptized by John. The human community, which John personifies, is involved in the event. The Holy Spirit overshadows Jesus, who becomes aware that he is the source of the Spirit for all men. We know that «In the beginning was the Word,» and that all things are in the Word. But this is the human nature of Jesus experiencing and hearing those beautiful words: «This is my beloved Son in whom I am well pleased.» What has he done in Nazareth for thirty years to warrant such approbation? He has been Son. It is more important to be than to do, but now he must do. The Spirit leads him into the desert.

The contemplation on the sixth day is concerned with the temptations of Christ in the desert. [161] It is an extremely important contemplation and a very difficult part of Scripture because one has to grapple with literary genre, exegetical difficulties, and the theological questions about Christ's humanity as it comes into play in responding to these temptations. Most exegetes speak of Jesus as the «author» of the New Testament — «author» in the sense, not that he wrote or dictated it, but that the risen Jesus was present to the apostles and the early church as the New Testament was formed. The exegetes suggest that our Lord sees himself as the Second Israel.

Christ is tempted at two moments of great decision, at the beginning of his life of public witness to the Father and at the moment of acceptance of the Father's will in the garden of Gethsemane. The devil left him to return at the appointed time, says Luke. (Lk 4:13) In Matthew's account (Mt 4:1-11) the temptations are presented much as Ignatius does in the «Two Standards,» that is, in the sequence of riches, honors, and pride.

The temptations of Christ show that he is experiencing the force of evil and the force of suggestion, both from without and from within, in this time of decision. There are the questions from within: «What do these words of the Father, 'This is my beloved Son,' mean? What is my vocation? To what am I called for Israel, for the world?» Then possibly the exterior temptations from physical weakness and from the lure of the world about him as the devil presents it — riches, honors, power.

Thus, he anguishes through the temptations of Israel in the desert, experiencing his own life as a development of the history of Israel in the Old Testament. We know that Israel was tempted three times in the desert and succumbed every time; Jesus is tempted three times and does not fall. In him «we have one who has been tempted in every way that we are, though he is without sin.» (Heb 4:15)

The contemplation of the seventh day is also a decision making topic. It is the call and response of the apostles. Ignatius's points are certainly encouraging for one trying to choose a state of life:

Three other points must also be considered: 1. That the Apostles were uneducated and from a humble condition of life. 2. The dignity to which they were so gently called. 3. The gifts and graces by which they were raised above all the Fathers of the Old and New Testaments. [275]

In his points for the contemplation of the eighth day, «The Sermon on the Mount,» Ignatius wants the retreatant to place himself with the disciples as Christ «proposes the eight beatitudes... exhorts them to use their talents ... and commands [them] to love [their] enemies: 'I say, love your enemies, do good to them that hate you'.» [278]

Similarly, the ninth day's contemplation is to encourage one who is making a difficult decision for Christ. It is Christ walking on the waters towards the apostles' boat in a storm. «Christ says to them, 'It is I, fear not.' St. Peter at His command walked upon the waters ... he began to sink. Christ saved him.» [280]

The tenth day's contemplation is also pointed towards a following of Christ, but here it is the rejected Christ. After preaching in the temple each day, and «After His teaching, since there was no one in Jerusalem who would receive Him, He returned to Bethania.» [288]

The eleventh day's contemplation brings encouragement to follow a leader who can even raise Lazarus from the dead «by a command, 'Lazarus, come forth'.» [285]

The last contemplation Ignatius assigns for the «Second Week» is on the events of Palm Sunday. The people hail Jesus as a great leader. On this day they have joined him enthusiastically: «Hosanna to the Son of David! Blessed is he that cometh in the name of the Lord! Hosanna in the highest!» [287]

It appears that the exercitant is asked to decide his state

of life while contemplating other persons' considerations on a state of life. They are contemplations on Christ's life which illustrate a time of decision for Christ himself and for those who follow him.

The method of making decisions outside a retreat situation also demands freedom and prayer. It was Ignatius's practice to pray for an hour each day before Mass. It was during Mass itself that he often experienced the confirmation of decisions he had made in prayer. In his *Spiritual Journal* Ignatius recorded the consolations he had experienced, mostly with tears, when he was trying to decide specific points concerning the Jesuit Constitutions. The Eucharist is the ideal place to bring decisions because Christ is sacramentally present.

But the decision itself should not dominate the prayer. Rather, an individual should simply place himself in the presence of the mystery. For example, perhaps he may feel great anguish about setting up an apostolate and wish to seek help in prayer. The contemplation which he chooses may have nothing directly to do with this decision, but he finds peace and consolation in it. Or he may be thinking about leaving a position he holds, and in his prayer he places himself with the Lord going down the Jordan valley — and experiences consolation.

It is important to remember that the directives of Ignatius for choosing a state of life are to be used in the prayer context he gives — contemplation of select passages in the public life of Jesus. The simplicity of the technique is impressive, but we should also be aware of the spiritual difficulties that it involves.

The basic difficulty is to attain detachment from one's egotistical drives and to maintain a close union with Jesus. Such detachment and union are possible only through prayer and grace. Then comes the difficulty of avoiding the deceptions and evil suggestions that may arrive from outside oneself. Finally, to recognize and accept the movement of the Spirit towards a specific state of life may cause further trouble.

These difficulties and the directives given by Ignatius to overcome them, clearly indicate that choosing a state of life involves much more than an intellectual acceptance of what the gospels present. The heart of man must also respond: «*Cor ad cor loquitur.*» The whole person is involved. It is the response of his entire self to the personal invitation of Christ.

Ignatius presumes that the individual will experience affective movements which he can reflect upon and judge. The director is to help him in this task of reflection and judgment. But the exercitant alone can say with certainty whether the Lord wants him to make a particular choice.

Sometimes the Lord's way is in sharp contrast to all the person's past life, yet it brings order out of chaos: it is a moment of conversion. At other times the person comes to recognize that his whole life had been moving this way, and he notices how his whole being harmonizes with this way. Then a certitude arises that he cannot doubt. He understands the Lord's words: «the sheep follow because they know his voice. ... I am the good shepherd; I know my own and my own know me, just as the Father knows me and I know the Father.» (Jn 10:4,14,15)

CHAPTER 14

SUFFERING WITH JESUS CHRIST

Blessed be the God and Father of our Lord Jesus Christ, a gentle Father and the God of all consolations, who comforts us in all our sorrows, so that we can offer others, in their sorrows, the consolation that we have received from God ourselves. Indeed, as the sufferings of Christ overflow to us, so, through Christ, does our consolation overflow. When we are made to suffer, it is for your consolation and salvation. When, instead, we are comforted, this should be a consolation to you, supporting you in patiently bearing the same sufferings as we bear. And our hope for you is confident, since we know that, sharing in our sufferings, you will also share our consolations. (2 Co 1:3-7)

Usually this section of Scripture is used for the «Fourth Week» because it ties in beautifully with the resurrection and helps us to understand our place with the Lord in bringing consolation to other people. But the point of sharing sufferings and consolation also applies to the «Third Week.» By this stage the retreatant has usually reached a decision made according to the «Rules of Discernment.» In the «Third Week» he is seeking confirmation of his decision and the strength to live by that decision.

In this spirit he prays the *Anima Christi.* Today the «Third Week» may be more meaningful than in the past because we have become more conscious of the humanity of Christ, and in the passion we see his humanity most vividly. We see Christ shaken by fear and suffering. It is quite easy, then, to identify with Christ in this phase of the Exercises.

A thought came to me recently as I celebrated the Eucharist. As he pours a little water into the wine, the priest says the following prayer: «By the mystery of this water and wine, may we come to share in Christ's divinity who humbled himself to share in our humanity.» This sentiment is present in both these last weeks of the Exercises. In the «Third Week» Ignatius says, «consider how the divinity hides itself.» [196] And in the «Fourth,» «consider the divinity... appearing and manifesting itself.» [223] Maybe it could be expressed in this way: «See how the glorified humanity presents itself in the resurrection; see how these extraordinary powers given to Christ do not operate in the passion.»

Thus, in the «Third Week» Christ is seen most clearly as a human being like us. He shared all our limitations, all our imperfections, «completely like his brothers... though he is without sin.» (Heb 2:17; 4:15) He knows fear, perhaps deeper fear than we do, because he himself has protected us from the object of that fear. Moreover, strange as it may seem, we have experienced the resurrection and he had not. He had not yet passed through death, but in baptism we have passed through it already.

The «Third and Fourth Weeks» taken together may be considered the unitive way, for the grace being sought is union with Christ, first in his suffering and then in his glory. [cf. 167] The unitive way is the stage in the spiritual life when we move out of ourselves towards Christ. In much the same way Jesus moved out of himself all through the passion. He is the man for others; he forgets himself. He is concerned about his apos-

232

tles: «If I am the one you are looking for, let these others go.» (Jn 18:8) He moves out to Pilate, trying to reach him. He comforts the women on the way of the cross. He pardons the good thief. He provides for the care of Mary and John as they stand at the foot of the cross. The grace to be sought, then, is the grace to move out of oneself, to be united with Christ in his suffering and later, in the «Fourth Week,» with Christ in his glory. Compassion demands that outward movement.

A number of the phrases used by Ignatius are very poignant. For example, «When Judas had gone out to sell his Lord,» [191] and «In this way I will labor through all the points.» [195] The theme of laboring with Christ, first presented in the «Kingdom» meditation, [95] is applied in this week of union: we are to labor with Christ in his suffering.

Once again Ignatius recommends that the retreatant's prayer take the form of contemplation. He is to contemplate the events of the passion in order to find an interior sense of suffering because Christ suffered so much for him. Jesus suffers for each man. Since he is Lord of the universe and the second Adam, his sufferings have a universal meaning. But his suffering on the cross is also for each man alone. Accordingly the retreatant prays for union with Christ in his suffering. As in the «Third Kind of Humility,» he prays that he may actively accept the suffering given to him by God the Father. The reason why he can ask for this grace is simply that Christ suffered for him — «My love is crucified.» But this is also a purifying and freeing experience, this desire to suffer with Christ in his suffering.

The contemplations of the «Third Week» are intended to help a man to escape his narrow self, to die to himself. This demands a deeply personal union with Christ in his suffering. Therefore, Ignatius has the exercitant seek the grace of «sorrow with Christ in sorrow, anguish with Christ in anguish, tears and

deep grief because of the great affliction Christ endures for me.»
[203] He asks for the grace to be pulled out of himself.

In dying to himself through union with Christ in his suffering, he gains strength and courage, freedom and conviction — all those graces that are necessary for those who wish to do the will of the Lord. Thus, in the contemplations of the passion he hopes to be present at the mysteries as no mere unimpassioned observer but rather as one who truly suffers with Christ. He asks to be drawn out of himself and taken up into the suffering of Jesus. It is a further entrance into the «Kingdom» meditation, where he sought to be with his leader.

This kind of prayer partakes of the nature of the unitive way rather than of the purgative way. The contemplations are quite different from the colloquy of the «First Exercise of the First Week.» In that colloquy the exercitant was a sinner seeking sorrow and forgiveness for his sins. In the «Third Week» he seeks to be sorrowful with Christ in his sorrow. He hopes to join Christ in saying «Yes» to the Father and «to make up all that has still to be undergone by Christ for the sake of his body, the Church.» (Col 1:24)

The «Third Week» raises the question of human suffering and divine providence: how can the providence of God permit the sufferings of men in this world? Of course, it is a mystery rather than a problem. Our limited humanity is constantly going through change. Earlier we discussed the relationship between suffering and man's sins, his disorder, his moral imperfections. Now, this relationship does not imply that the individual man necessarily causes his own physical suffering by his own sins. But the totality of evil perpetrated by the human race somehow has brought about physical suffering even for the innocent.

The question that might be asked is: «Why does God allow sin?» We might answer in human terms that it is a gamble on the part of God, a risk. We might say it is the «faith» of God in the sense that he knows how greatly freedom and love outweigh the evils of suffering and death. The freedom which is necessary for love raises man and glorifies him. It gives him a divine dimension which survives and transcends the downward pull of suffering and death. We might say that God gives man his freedom so that man can love and that, when he gives man freedom, he simultaneously gives him the possibility of sinning. He allows for the possibility of sinning. He allows for the possibility of evil because evil in the world is the result of man's selfishness. Even biological and physical evils are often the result of man's selfishness, greed, hatred, and desire to dominate.

Much of this is revealed in the life of Jesus Christ. Jesus is love incarnate; his reason for being is love. He is the revelation in human form of God's love for man. He teaches us that God the Father is love and that man's nature is fulfilled in love for other men as the expression of his love for God. Jesus is the being whose total life force is love. What we see in Jesus is that in the moment of suffering this love triumphs over sin, suffering, and death. Love is greater than death.

Not only does Christ triumph over sin, suffering and death, but he becomes the instrument for us also to triumph over sin, suffering and death. Through his contact with us in the Spirit, he gives us the courage and the strength to triumph, not only over sin, suffering and death, but even over the fear of these evils. It follows that bitterness is a non-Christian reaction and an unbelieving response.

Christ's death on the cross is an example and a living force for us. He gives us the willingness to die on a cross for our fellow man. Like him we are to relieve the sufferings of other people, psychological or spiritual. People ought to be fed and clothed

235

and sheltered — it is part of the Christian vocation to seek this. If we can help freely and humbly to feed, clothe and shelter other people, we are losing some of our selfishness and moving out of ourselves after the example of Christ. Down through the centuries the Church through her hospitals and congregations for ransoming of captives has made an effort to relieve physical and mental suffering. Nevertheless, the mystery of the passion and its more important work is to bring meaning into the sufferings themselves.

There is an aspect of suffering that is very mysterious and that goes beyond what is merely physical. The message of the cross and the resurrection meets that deeper dimension of suffering. When discussing the «First Week,» I referred to a paper by Tillich, «You Are Accepted.» In that study Tillich shows how Christ's life demonstrates that we are accepted by God and that this meets the deeper suffering of all men: the need to be known, to be accepted, to be loved.

Christ's death on the cross and his resurrection from the dead is the ultimate expression of the fact that man is indeed accepted. His death on the cross is the great sign of his love and forgiveness. His resurrection is the sign that the Father accepts Christ and you and me. «Our faith too will be 'considered' if we believe in him who raised Jesus our Lord from the dead, Jesus who was *put to death for our sins* and raised to life to justify us.» (Rm 4:24, 25)

Lourdes is an example of what I am saying. There are millions of people who have gone to Lourdes over the years, and a number of physical cures and healings have taken place. But the message of Lourdes is that God is with us, and that suffering and death are not the end of this life. Many people have left Lourdes still suffering physically but able to sustain their suffering; a much greater miracle has taken place in the heart

236

of the person. Physical miracles help support our faith. But the basic miracle at Lourdes is the miracle of faith, the miracle of meaning. Thus, Christ's death and his resurrection are signs of the meaningfulness of life and the meaningfulness of suffering. Life and love go beyond all suffering.

Earlier, when discussing the colloquy with Christ hanging on the cross, I emphasized the importance of Jesus as personal savior. There in the «First Week» the retreatant begged for the grace of knowing that Jesus actually saves him from eternal death by his loving obedience to the Father. In contemplating the mysteries of the passion in the «Third Week,» however, what the retreatant seeks is the grace of union with Jesus in his suffering. This means an even deeper understanding of the personal savior through compassion. The desire to bear poverty, insults and wrongs with Christ, to which the retreatant was incited in the «Three Kinds of Humility,» can move to the level of experience when the grace of compassion is received. He is now given a new form of freedom. He is saved, not only from his sins, but even from the self-centered fears that prevent him from loving as he might desire. The grace of union with Christ in his suffering draws him out of himself so effectively that he fully recognizes Jesus as the one who enables him, not only to live, but even to love. (*cf.* Rm 4:25 — 5:11)

The passage quoted at the beginning of this chapter expresses our main work as Christians today: we must counter those philosophies of despair that say that death is the end of all. The Christian must even question the optimistic humanist who holds that death is the end of all but argues that man may still live a loving, peaceful life here on earth by means of reason alone. Without the foundation of Christ and the ultimate meaning of his death and resurrection, it is very hard to convince anyone that he should live a loving, peaceful life. Moreover, without

Christ he can't even fulfill such good desires. The only reason a man has for going out of himself to the extreme of suffering and dying for others is to be found in Jesus Christ.

Contemplating the passion of our Lord can be an excruciating experience. The grace one is seeking is a deep-felt sense of the sufferings of our Lord «for me.» This desire can cause interior pain for two reasons. The first is one's natural fear of his own possible sufferings for Christ. The second arises from his close union to the person of the suffering Lord.

The «Agony in the Garden» is a central mystery for these two reasons. For in contemplating the «Agony» one is present with Jesus as he experiences fear of the physical suffering entailed in his commitment to the Father. And with Jesus he might cry out, «Take this chalice away from me.» He is also present with Jesus as he seeks love and support from his disciples. In both his fear of physical suffering and his need for human love, Jesus experiences the weakness felt by a human being before the sufferings involved in a total commitment to God. In his trial he turns to his apostles for love, but he finds them asleep. Then he prays again to his Father to remove the sufferings enjoined by his commitment. The Father answers his prayer, not by removing the sufferings or the need for love, but by strengthening Christ with his own love, the Holy Spirit.

This contemplation on Christ's need for love in the garden of Gethsemane can be especially helpful for people who are caught up in emotional involvements which their vocational commitment (in marriage or a religious order) does not permit. It is encouraging to realize that Jesus also felt the need of support from his apostles and that he brought about the redemption of the world through «prayer and entreaty, aloud and in silent tears, to the one who had the power to save him out of death, and he submitted so humbly that his prayer was heard.

Although he was Son, he learnt to obey through suffering.» (Heb 5:7, 8) When contemplating this and the other mysteries of the passion, a person can find the freedom to give himself fully to his commitment.

Counseling someone who is struggling to overcome an emotional involvement of this sort requires an unusual degree of sympathy, understanding and patience. The counselee should not deny the reality of his human affections and sexual drives. In fact, it sometimes helps if he can sincerely thank God for them. In the severe «Agony» that he suffered, Jesus reacted with deeply felt emotion — there was no denial of the truth. Often it is only through union with Christ in this contemplation that a retreatant can learn to handle the loneliness and pain he experiences at the time of separating himself from a wrongful love relationship.

The prayer of Jesus, «Not my will but Thine be done,» must also be the prayer of one who is caught up in an emotional relationship with another. It is therefore important to discover the actual state of the person's commitment to his vows. If a deep commitment is there, then counseling is possible. Through prayer and discernment the person may realize that the very fear of falling in love is often worse than falling in love itself.

The fear of sinning can be more enslaving than the sin because fear implies an unwillingness to stand free, an unwillingness to grow fully human. Of course, prudence (in a mature and well-balanced person) will know the difference between silly recklessness and sensible human relationships, but prudence is too often interpreted in a negative way alone: it inhibits rather than encourages true action.

This fearful attitude betrays a lack of trust in God. Religious people who are filled with such fear are usually perfectionists or puritans, somewhat inhuman — and hard to live with. It follows that the first problem to deal with is fear. When fear has been mitigated or overcome, then the person may be able to think more responsibly about the one he has fallen in love with; he must come to feel true concern for the other person's union with Christ.

Similarly, prayer and discernment will enable a man to distinguish «falling in love» from «having a love affair.» To enter into an illicit love affair usually implies a calculated step, a definite decision, at some stage in the relationship. And this step proceeds from selfish motives of one kind or another. It means an acceptance of those motives, a deadening of conscience, a refusal that leads to hardness of heart.

But to fall in love may come upon a person unawares, when busy with other matters, or when his guard is down because of besetting troubles. Perhaps he has been foolishly imprudent, but he has not selfishly chosen it; rather, he finds himself suddenly caught in its grip.

If there has been no intimate expression of love, spiritual direction may be complicated by another sort of fear — fear concerning the loss of chastity or of singleness of heart as an apostle of Christ. At other times an individual may fear losing the love of the other person. Such fears can be painful and can place serious obstacles in the way of spiritual growth. While maintaining his reverence for the other, the counselee must somehow gain freedom from his fears.

Sometimes, especially if the other party is married and has children, the only solution is to break off the relationship. At other times, especially if intimacy and sexual intercourse have been avoided, some kind of friendship might be maintained. Nevertheless, the motivation must not be fear but rather responsible love (although prudential fear may be right in certain cases). The relationship can be cooled down if both persons are devoting themselves to the Father in union with Christ. This usually means getting involved in apostolic efforts in separation from each other so that the grace of their vocation can operate. As in all love relationships, there will be anguish. But if Christ's agony is kept before one's eyes, the vocation can be lived.

Once the counselee reveals his anguish to you, he often finds new hope because he discovers that he is accepted, if only by his counselor. He discovers that, after all, he has not destroyed the world by falling in love with this man or woman. That idea is only another form of fear. But as long as the liaison remains hidden, it cannot be handled. When revealed to the light, Christ's love and truth can work.

Sometimes a sister may have fallen into sexual sin with a man she did not really love; afterwards she becomes extremely upset and wonders whether she should not leave religious life. Here again she needs to accept her humanity. She needs to accept her sin in all humility. She probably thinks that her virginity and consecration have been destroyed. Yet, especially if she receives good direction, she can obtain great graces of humility and great appreciation of the Lord's special love for her, and thus she may end by consecrating herself more completely to the Lord. But first she must face the fact of her selfishness and then, with the help of God, come to realize that the Lord still loves her. And if others in the same community know about it and accept her, through them she can experience very realistically the acceptance of God himself.

That the fear of falling in love is often worse than falling in love can sometimes be seen in the apostolate. This fear will inhibit one's self-expression and adversely affect one's apostolate. Yet to take the necessary precautions is a sign not of fear but of wisdom. Usually when a celibate becomes emotionally

241

involved with another, some previous cause has disposed him for it: too heavy a work load may have drained his spirit; he may have abandoned old habits of prayer without developing new ones; a cold community may have left him isolated affectively; through changes in our culture and in the Church, feelings of insecurity may have intensified in him; one or more of these causes, or a combination of other factors, may be at the root of his trouble. They help to explain the depth of his emotional involvement.

Since reasons of this sort are usually present, it is not always helpful to say to him at once, «Break off the relationship.» His involvement, however ambiguous it is, may be the sole support he has at the moment. He must re-establish his life upon a firm basis — that is the essential requirement. In the meantime his relationship should be cooled somewhat, and for this he will need sympathetic understanding and real help for his root problems. If he succeeds in regaining emotional balance and self-control, his true vocation will eventually reassert itself.

It is important in directing such persons to see that they reflect frankly upon the deeper causes and effects of such emotional involvements. Possibly they will discover that a sinful desire to control another person is at the heart of the relationship. Perhaps the experience they have undergone will highlight the grace of humility. They may come to realize their inability to control their emotional life and so be led to the humble acceptance of their creaturehood.

This is only one example of union with Christ in his suffering. There are obviously as many other applications as there are believers. But the «Third Week» can bring a new perspective even to the excruciating suffering that begins with innocent friendship but ends in a compromising love-relationship. If by these contemplations we achieve union with Christ in his suf-

242

fering, they will draw us out of ourselves and make us instruments of his grace for others.

CHAPTER 15

JOY WITH JESUS CHRIST RISEN

Blessed be God the Father of our Lord Jesus Christ, who in his great mercy has given us a new birth as his sons, by raising Jesus Christ from the dead, so that we have a sure hope and the promise of an inheritance that can never be spoilt or soiled and never fade away, because it is being kept for you in the heavens. Through your faith, God's power will guard you until the salvation which has been prepared is revealed at the end of time. This is a cause of great joy for you, even though you may for a short time have to bear being plagued by all sorts of trials; so that, when Jesus Christ is revealed, your faith will have been tested and proved like gold — only it is more precious than gold, which is corruptible even though it bears testing by fire — and then you will have praise and glory and honor. You did not see him, yet you love him; and still without seeing him, you are already filled with a joy so glorious that it cannot be described, because you believe; and you are sure of the end to which your faith looks forward, that is, the salvation of your souls. (1 P 1:3-9)

The resurrection of the body is a great mystery. We have no idea whatsoever about the resurrected state of man. We know it is a new way of living. In the appearance to Thomas and the other apostles, Jesus says: «Put your finger here; look, here are my hands. Give me your hand; put it into my side,» and «have you anything here to eat?» But the apostles look back at him, Scripture tells us, without being sure about him and without wanting to ask, «Who are you?» They know who he is, but somehow feel that he is different.

What is meant by this resurrected body is still unknown to us. In his first letter to the Church in Corinth, Paul faced that problem early in the Church's life. He compares the body to a grain of seed sown in the ground, where it dies and brings forth something quite different, a plant. (1 Co 15:36-44) As a plant differs from its seed, so our risen bodies will differ from our present bodies. This analogy stresses the change that must be expected, but it sheds no light on what the risen body will be like.

What matters, however, is that the human person will continue to exist. And because Jesus is human as well as divine, we must conclude that his body and soul continue. In a new philosophy of man, we would not concern ourselves with the body-soul division, but would emphasize the fact that in Christ's risen life his humanity is fully realized.

Moreover, in the resurrection Christ continues to be present to his apostles, and present in his entire humanity. This, of course, is the reason why they can recall and celebrate his death with joy and gratitude in every liturgy of the Eucharist. The Eucharist becomes the occasion for his real sacramental presence among them and among us.

In the fifth point of the «Fourth Week» Ignatius wants us to «Consider the office of consoler that Christ our Lord exercises, and compare it with the way in which friends are wont to console each other.» [224] This is a beautiful way of showing how Jesus goes about bringing joy and hope and confidence to people. In all of his resurrection appearances the basic theme given is the *Emmanuel* theme, the continuation of the Incarnation today. God continues with us and is present to us.

The first contemplation of the «Fourth Week» centers on Jesus's apparition to his mother. In explaining this contemplation Ignatius provides the pattern for all the contemplations that follow. [226] In the first prelude he notes that Christ's body is reunited with his soul and divinity. This echoes back to the contemplation for Holy Saturday in the «Third Week.» In both places Ignatius expresses things differently than we might today (we would prefer to speak of man as a unity). Ignatius writes: «after Jesus expired on the cross His body remained separated from the soul, but always united with the divinity. His soul, likewise united with the divinity, descended into hell. There He sets free the souls of the just, then comes to the sepulcher, and rising, appears in body and soul to His Blessed Mother.» [219] While the language used here may not satisfy us, the theological basis is solid enough. The main point is that, after rising in his total humanity, he appeared to his mother. Nor does it matter whether it was on Good Friday night, on Saturday morning, or on Sunday morning. We would probably be wise to stick to Sunday as the day of the first appearance since this conforms more closely to the Scriptural data.

Ignatius is well aware that this mystery is not recorded in scripture, [299] but it is only natural that Christ should appear to his mother first because he loved her: «He was her first born son.» Some theologians say he did not have to appear to his mother because her faith did not need such an appearance. This seems to miss the point: Jesus wanted to appear to his mother in order to share with her his joy and glory.

The grace of these days, like that of the «Third Week,» is to move beyond oneself and become united with Christ: «to be glad and rejoice intensely because of the great joy and the glory

246

of Christ our Lord.» [221] This truly means escaping from one's narrow self to an unusual degree.

Some people in fact have difficulty moving out of the «Third Week» into the «Fourth Week» because of their profound sense of identification with Christ in his passion. The director should be sensitive to this problem and try to find out why the person experiences difficulty. If it proceeds from a legitimate religious need, then it may be good to keep him in the «Third Week» a little longer — it is after all, a genuine part of the unitive way. Otherwise, for someone who finds the transition to the «Fourth Week» difficult, the best resurrection event to begin with might be the apparition to Magdalene. She also continues to cling to the earthly and suffering Lord: «Sir, if you have taken him away, tell me where you have put him.» (Jn 20:15) She is still holding on to a thing, to the dead Christ perhaps, or better, to the resuscitated Christ, who would be similar to Lazarus brought back to life, (Jn 11:43, 44) rather than the resurrected, glorified Christ. The apparition to Magdalen can be the instrument to lead this person into the «Fourth Week.»

In the resurrection appearances we hear Christ's command: «Don't stand there. Go and tell the brethren.» The message of the resurrection is «go and spread the good news.» In other words, get out of yourself; go and tell other people. But a director has to let this imperative arise out of the individual's own prayer.

From the commands Jesus later gave to Thomas, we realize that Jesus had actually been present when Thomas declared his disbelief in the resurrection and laid down his conditions. But a week later the Lord comes to him and takes pity on him. The risen Jesus presents himself in all humility before the doubter. How Thomas must have prayed in his desolation, separated for a week from the believing community!

Volumes could be written about the resurrection appearances. But this would require a set of points on each one of them. Interestingly, what was said in the «Call of the King» about the person called, «that by following me in suffering, he may follow me in glory,» [95] is now expressed to the disciples on the way to Emmaus: «Was it not ordained that Christ should suffer and so enter into his glory?» (Lk 24:26) Again in this resurrection account we see the desolation of the two men, who would not believe the women or their community. And we notice how easily Christ is hidden or unrecognizable to those who are in desolation. He does not seem to be present.

Another interesting note is that it is through Scripture that he instructs them. We see how delicately Christ teaches these disciples: he never wishes to overpower their freedom. Thus Christ waits for the disciples to invite him in. Once they have made this gesture of love, then he reveals himself to them and they know him in the breaking of the bread. The Eucharistic motif is dominant in many of the resurrection appearances. Here, as elsewhere, the effect of consolation is to make the disciples rush back to Jerusalem with the good news.

Christ's return to the Father in the mystery of the Ascension results in the sending of the Spirit to us. The indwelling Spirit, as has been emphasized so often in these pages, is the one who brings Christ's freeing action to each one of us. This life-giving Spirit prays in us, (Rm 8:26) giving us both the desire and the will. (Ph 2:13) It is he who makes it possible for Christ to relive in us all the events of his earthly life and thus, in contemplation, make us present to his mysteries. It is likewise he who makes it possible for us to love others as Christ and the Father loved us and thus bring about that unity of love among men which we express and hope for in the Eucharist. Jesus's Spirit is a life-giving spirit poured into our hearts to make us, and all things, new.

In the scene on the shore of Lake Tiberias, we see how this newness is presented: it is the same lake, the same fishermen, the same miraculous catch of fish, the same Peter, yet all is different now. Thus it is when the joy of Christ becomes our joy — we can truly appreciate the words of Revelation: «You see this city? Here God lives among men. He will make *his home among them; they shall be his people,* and he will be their God; his name is *God-with-them. He will wipe away all tears from their eyes;* there will be no death, and no more mourning or sadness. The world of the past has gone.» (Rv 21:3, 4)

And in the final appearance before Christ ascends to his Father, we are conscious that the scenes are the same as on Holy Thursday night: the upper room, the meal, the walk to the Mount of Olives, but now everything is new.

The «Contemplation to Attain Love of God».

This, then, is what I pray, kneeling before the Father, from whom every family, whether spiritual or natural, takes its name:

Out of his infinite glory, may he give you the power through his Spirit for your hidden self to grow strong, so that Christ may live in your hearts through faith, and then, planted in love and built on love, you will with all the saints have strength to grasp the breadth and the length, the height and the depth; until, knowing the love of Christ, which is beyond all knowledge, you are filled with the utter fullness of God.

Glory be to him whose power, working in us, can do infinitely more than we can ask or imagine; glory be to him from generation to generation in the Church and in Christ Jesus for ever and ever. Amen. (Eph 3:14-21)

All of us may wish to love God with the totality of our being, but we know that we do not do it. God loves us, but how can we love God? We realize that we need a method of prayer to do this and Ignatius gives us one. It is a «Contemplation to Attain Love of God.»

Ignatius supplies two prenotes. «The first is that love ought to manifest itself in deeds rather than words.» [230] «The second is that love consists in a mutual sharing of goods.» [231] These two notes are examples of God's action in the four points Ignatius gives in the contemplation itself. [234-237]

«Love manifests itself in deeds» is not a pelagian statement. The pelagian's assumption is that he must prove by works that he loves God. In the statement of Ignatius, however, love is presupposed before the deeds. Man's deeds do not earn God's love.

When our love overflows in deeds, we become aware of the presence of love. We have an objective experience of God loving in and through us. It is a remarkable event to experience ourselves loving in the Christian manner — loving our enemies, doing good to those who hate us. Where does it come from? There is only one source for this kind of love — Jesus Christ himself.

Mutual sharing has become the way to describe the experience of life and love today. It is even seen as the source for building a community of love. To share oneself on the deepest level is to share one's faith, one's love for God, one's hope in Christ.

Ignatius's method for loving God is really very simple.

Of course, it is dependent on grace: «Here it will be to ask for an intimate knowledge of the many blessings received, that filled with gratitude for all, I may in all things love and serve the Divine Majesty.» [233] The method itself is simply to deepen our appreciation for the gifts the Lord has given.

If we have a deep-felt appreciation of God's goodness to us, this gratitude is already an expression of love. And as we ponder on the events of our life, we become conscious with Paul that all is gift. (*cf.* 1 Co 4:7; Eph 2:4-6) But the petition moves beyond thanksgiving to thankfully giving ourselves in return — to serve, to practical love. We are to move from an attitude of thanks to one of welcome, «For all that has been, thank you Lord. For all that will be, Yes!»

Ignatius then suggests four points to help us pray. These points only exemplify the sharing act of God with man. They are truly personal to each man as he becomes aware that the totality of the Lord is focusing in on him. The phrase in the first point that is most impressive is this one: «and finally, how much, as far as He can, the same Lord desires to give Himself to me according to His divine decrees.» [234] We cannot help but recall the longing of the heart of Christ for the love of men and the fact that his love is so often rejected by them. (*cf.* Jn 1:1-14; Lk 2:34; 4:29)

The language used by Ignatius also expands upon his description of sharing: «for example, the lover gives and shares with the beloved what he possesses. ... knowledge ... honors, or riches.» [231]For it is not just a matter of sharing his possessions but of sharing himself. The freedom to receive or reject this self-offering of the Lord is an awesome thing. These words also stress the fact that grace is the self-communication of the persons of the Trinity to man in love.

The second point emphasizes the closeness of God-with-us,

the indwelling of the Holy Spirit. Paul makes much of this truth in his letters. (*cf.* Eph 3:20; Rm 8:9; Ga 2:20) The immanence of God in his creatures is presented in all four points of the contemplation, and this is how the final exercise differs from the «Principle and Foundation,» which shows God in his more transcendent nature. This point may also suggest why Ignatius does not include any contemplation on the events of Pentecost. (Ac 2:1-41) To grow aware of the Spirit working in man and drawing him gently but persistently to the Father's love in Jesus Christ has been one purpose of all the Exercises. The Spirit himself is *the* gift.

The third point reminds one again of the «Kingdom» meditation [95] and the contemplation on the «Nativity.» [116] One might say that the Trinity is the prime example of a contemplative in action as the Three Persons look down on the whole earth, [102] and the Father and Holy Spirit send the Son to labor for mankind.

The fourth point emphasizes the truth that God is the source of all that is good in the world and in men. We may recall the «Second Exercise» of the «First Week,» where Ignatius bids the retreatant contrast himself with God. [59] But in the present contemplation we realize how God comes down to us, and we are reminded of those passages in the Old Testament which describe God as a Father stooping down to lift up his little child. (Dt 1:31; Ps 40:1)

After reflecting on each point, Ignatius suggests the exercitant should make the offering of himself in the terms of the famous prayer, «Take, Lord, and Receive.» [234] This offering sometimes frightens people to the extent that the whole «Contemplation to Attain Love of God» becomes unreal to them. But they have mistakenly approached it as if it were a contract arrangement: «I offer this to you if you will give your grace.»

And so they have felt compelled to screw up their courage to face, for example, the possibility of insanity as part of the contract! But if this offering is approached in the Biblical way of a covenant relationship with the Lord, it is much more meaningful.

In the counseling situation, as has been emphasized already, fear is the sign of the evil one. In a similar way here, one runs up against the fear that comes with the offering of oneself unconditionally to God. It has often been unwisely compared to writing a blank check. The experience of covenant is much different from fulfilling a business contract. It involves the sharing of oneself and all that one has with another.

The great covenant is that of the Lord with his people; He is always faithful to His promises. The wedding covenant and religious vows find their source and mood in the covenant of the Lord. Accordingly, «Take, Lord, and Receive» starts from a recognition that the Lord has shared everything, including himself, with the exercitant; the exercitant desires that this sharing should continue to grow until the Spirit stirs up in him the longing to share with God all that he has and is. He wants to live in the present all God's loving acts of the past. He wants to share all in Christ's name: «where two or three meet in my name, I shall be there with them.» (Mt 18:20)

Through the Holy Spirit dwelling in man, this offering becomes the means to a participation in the love of the Trinity. It is a love that can be expressed as a sharing and an offering of one person to the other in the Godhead. Thus, the Father offers himself in the Word and through the Word to all creation, to Mary, to every created person. And the Son, who is the Word made flesh, receiving all, offers it back to the Father himself in the Word and in all creatures. And this giving and receiving of persons is the very person of the Spirit, the full expression of free-covenanted-love. The Spirit gives himself to those free beings (men) and moves them to share in the love relationship of the Trinity.

The contemplation itself can be the basis of all prayer for the contemplative in action who returns to the scene of his daily activities. In spiritual direction, it can become the pivotal point for self-awareness and self-realization in freedom, the covenant-relationship with the Lord that underlies every choice, flows into every act, finds God in all persons and in all things.

REFERENCES

1. All quotations of *The Spiritual Exercises of St. Ignatius* are taken from the translation of Louis Puhl, Chicago: Loyola University Press, 1951. At the end of each quotation, the numbers of sections given in this edition are enclosed in square brackets and inserted in the text.

2. All Scriptural quotations are taken from *The Jerusalem Bible*, New York: Doubleday, 1966.

3. Harriot, John, «Himself He Cannot Save,» *The Way*, 10 (1970), 318-26.

4. Rahner, Karl, *Spiritual Exercises*, New York: Herder and Herder, 1965.

5. Maslow, Abraham, *Religion, Values, and Peak Experiences*, New York: Viking Press, 1970.

6. *Cf. Theology Digest*, 10 (1960), 45-46.

7. Malatesta et al., *Discernment of Spirits*, Collegeville, Minn.: 1970.

8. *Cf.* especially Kyne, Michael, *Supplement to The Way*, 6 (1968), 20-26.

9. *Sacramentum Mundi*, Vol. 2, New York: Herder and Herder, 1968.

10. Rahner, Karl, *The Dynamic Element in the Church*, Montreal, Herder, 1964.

11. Stanley, David, «Contemplation of the Gospel, Ignatius Loyola, and The Contemporary Christian,» *Theological Studies*, 29, (1968), 417-43.

12. Whelan, Joseph, «Contemplating Christ,» *The Way,* 10 (1970), 187-98.

13. Rahner, Hugo, *Ignatius the Theologian,* New York: Herder and Herder, 1968.

14. Metz, Johannes, *Poverty of Spirit,* Glen Rock, N.J.: Newman, 1968.

15. Roustang, François, *Growth in the Spirit,* New York: Sheed and Ward, 1966.

16. See the article by Charmot, François, «Discernment of Spirits and Spiritual Direction,» in *Finding God in All Things,* trans. and ed. William Young, Chicago: Henry Regnery, 1958.

17. *Cf.* Rahner, Karl, *Dynamic Element in the Church,* p. 152. The operative phrase, «and gives us a sense of himself,» is not found in Hugo Rahner's *Saint Ignatius Loyola: Letters to Woman,* (trans.) Kathleen Pond and S.A.H. Weetman, New York: Herder and Herder, 1960, p. 334. But the Spanish text in *Obras Completas de San Ignacio de Loyola,* Madrid: Biblioteca de Autores Cristianos, 1963, p. 627, has the phrase «*y nosotros a su sentido.*»